SCOTT FORESMAN

Art

Unit-by-Unit Resources

Grade 8

PEARSON
Scott
Foresman

Editorial Offices: Glenview, Illinois • Parsippany, New Jersey • New York, New York

Sales Offices: Parsippany, New Jersey • Duluth, Georgia • Glenview, Illinois • Coppell, Texas • Ontario, California • Mesa, Arizona

ISBN: 0-328-10552-X

4 5 6 7 8 9 10 V034 13 12 11 10 09 08 07 06

Table of Contents

Setting Up the Classroom 4

Storage Ideas 5

Ways to Display 6

Unit 1   Overview 7

     Materials List 8

     Family Letters 9

     Vocabulary Practice 1 11

     Vocabulary Practice 2 13

     Unit Test 15

     Answer Key 19

     Scoring Rubric 20

     Self-Check 21

     Curriculum Connection 23

     Culminating Activities 24

Unit 2   Overview 25

     Materials List 26

     Family Letters 27

     Vocabulary Practice 1 29

     Vocabulary Practice 2 31

     Unit Test 33

     Answer Key 37

     Scoring Rubric 38

     Self-Check 39

     Curriculum Connection 41

     Culminating Activities 42

Unit 3   Overview 43

     Materials List 44

     Family Letters 45

     Vocabulary Practice 1 47

     Vocabulary Practice 2 49

     Unit Test 51

     Answer Key 55

     Scoring Rubric 56

     Self-Check 57

     Curriculum Connection 59

     Culminating Activities 60

Unit 4 Overview 61

Materials List 62

Family Letters 63

Vocabulary Practice 1 65

Vocabulary Practice 2 67

Unit Test 69

Answer Key 73

Scoring Rubric 74

Self-Check 75

Curriculum Connection 77

Culminating Activities 78

Unit 5 Overview 79

Materials List 80

Family Letters 81

Vocabulary Practice 1 83

Vocabulary Practice 2 85

Unit Test 87

Answer Key 91

Scoring Rubric 92

Self-Check 93

Curriculum Connection 95

Culminating Activities 96

Unit 6 Overview 97

Materials List 98

Family Letters 99

Vocabulary Practice 1 101

Vocabulary Practice 2 103

Unit Test 105

Answer Key 109

Scoring Rubric 110

Self-Check 111

Curriculum Connection 113

Culminating Activities 114

Studio/Project Log 115

Venn Diagram 117

Two-Column Chart 118

Three-Column Chart 119

Flowchart 120

Setting Up the Classroom

A Creative Environment

A child's first and most meaningful artistic experiences often take place in the classroom. Here are a few ideas for creating interest and inspiration in the classroom:

- Decorate a bulletin board with textured fabrics or old hats.
- Display colorful travel posters and Fine Art Prints on classroom walls.
- Hang colorful kites or umbrellas from the ceiling in one part of the classroom, overlapping them for full coverage.
- Create a "color environment" by covering a wall with warm or cool colors that appear on a variety of fabrics, beach towels, quilts, ribbons, banners, fans, and so on.

Space Planning

Provide sufficient space to allow students to work on individual projects while sharing materials. Use ideas such as the following to adapt the classroom for art:

- Arrange desks in groups of four to form squares.
- Place groups of desks in a way that allows a regular flow of traffic to the teacher's desk, the storage area, and the clean-up areas.
- Provide tables in the rear of the room for working space, group work, or drying space.
- If possible, set up freestanding easels for drawing or painting studios or projects. The easels will eliminate the need for large amounts of desk space.

Distribution and Cleanup

Provide time at the beginning of the studio or project for distribution and at the end for cleanup. Here are some ideas to facilitate organized distribution and cleanup:

- To distribute materials, place them on empty tables, buffet-style. Have students wash their hands and then pick up the materials they need, or have one student from each group collect the materials that group members will need.
- Be sure that an adult distributes and collects materials that could pose a safety hazard.
- Assign a different clean-up job to each student in a group. For example, one student cleans paintbrushes, one student collects paints, one student places artworks on the drying rack, and one student collects trash and wipes desks.

Storage Ideas

Storing Materials

Following are some ideas for effective storage of art supplies, tools, and visual aids:

- Wear an apron with several pockets to hold items such as a stapler, tape, and scissors so that you have your own materials as you walk around the room to assist students.
- Store supplies and tools on a movable cafeteria cart with shelves or in plastic tote trays that can be placed in the middle of each group of students.
- Keep supplies such as chalk, crayons, and markers in labeled baby wipe boxes.
- Hang a pegboard panel with hooks behind your desk for tools such as wire cutters, scissors, and so on. Make an outline of each tool on the pegboard for easy inventory.
- Store photographs and magazine cutouts in hanging file folders organized by subject such as *buildings, insects, sculptures,* and so on.
- Obtain five-gallon utility buckets with lids for supplies such as clay, sand, and plaster.
- For easy marker storage, place marker caps, top down, in a tub of wet Plaster of Paris. Let dry. Have students return markers to the caps as they use them.
- Store paper or 3-D supplies in empty soda pop flats.
- When using shelf space to store materials, place like items on the same shelf, such as recyclables, fabric, and so on. Label each shelf area for easy distribution and cleanup.

Storing Works in Progress

Take the challenge out of storing works in progress by incorporating some of these ideas:

- Make a portfolio for each student by taping together two pieces of posterboard. Place artworks in the portfolios and store in alphabetical order in a cardboard storage box.
- Line three-dimensional artworks along the baseboard of the classroom.
- Talk to the custodian about "borrowing" closet space from another part of the school.
- Use a wooden clothes drying rack or a clothesline as a drying center.

Ways to Display

Hanging Displays

Displaying students' artworks can build self-esteem and encourage students to improve their skills. Try ideas such as the following to create pleasing hanging displays:

• Secure a fairly large bare tree branch in a five-gallon utility bucket with sand and Plaster of Paris. Use string and paper clips to hang small artworks from the limbs.

• Attach strings with paper clips to the ceiling. Hang artworks from the strings.

• Hang a clothesline across one wall. Attach artworks with clothespins.

• Cut open refrigerator boxes and arrange them accordion style. Cover the boxes with neutral butcher paper and attach completed artworks to these "gallery walls." Set them up in hallways or in the classroom.

• Obtain permission to adhere corkboard to cupboard doors, closet doors, or storage cabinet fronts. Attach artworks with tacks.

• Place matting behind hanging artworks whenever possible, so that adhesives are used on the mats rather than the artworks.

Surface Displays

To display three-dimensional artworks, use ideas such as the following:

• Tour the school to find interesting display locations such as trophy cases, shelves in the principal's office or library, front corners of a stage, or on shelves along the crown molding in hallways.

• Create extra table space by placing a sheet of plywood on top of utility buckets.

• Stack empty milk crates like bookcases. Cover the shelves with dark paper.

• When creating table displays, stack books at varying heights. Drape the table and books with dark fabric and arrange the artworks on the table and on top of the books.

• For small, light three-dimensional artworks, create display shelves by stapling shoebox lids upside down to a bulletin board. Place the artworks inside the lids.

Overview

Many prominent artists are featured in Unit 1, such as:

Frida Kahlo

Mexican painter

Frida Kahlo. *The Chicken,* 1945. Oil on masonite. Fundación Dolores Olmedo, Mexico City, Mexico.

Unit Contents

Materials List 8
Family Letter 9
Vocabulary Practice 1 11
Vocabulary Practice 2 13
Unit Test 15
Answer Key 19
Scoring Rubric 20
Self-Check 21
Curriculum Connection 23
Culminating Activities 24

Unit Vocabulary

1. elements of art, line, gesture drawing, actual lines, implied lines
2. shape, geometric shapes, organic shapes, tessellation
3. form, geometric forms, organic forms, sculpture, assemblages
4. space, positive space, negative space, depth, overlapping, foreground, background, middle ground
5. linear perspective, horizon line, vanishing point, atmospheric perspective, one-point perspective, two-point perspective
6. value, shading, contrast
7. color, primary colors, secondary color, intermediate colors, warm colors, cool colors
8. color scheme, monochromatic, analogous, complementary, neutral, tints, shades, intensity
9. texture, tactile texture, visual texture

Materials List

Below are materials needed for each studio experience and the portfolio project. Materials followed by an* are items families might be able to donate.

Studio 1: Gesture Drawing with Line

☐ 2 sheets of 12" × 18" newsprint per student
☐ soft-lead pencils or black crayons

Studio 2: Make a Tessellation

☐ 3" squares of posterboard
☐ colored pencils, non-toxic markers, or crayons
☐ tape
☐ scissors ⚠S
☐ 12" × 18" white drawing paper

Studio 3: Assemble a Form

☐ drawing paper
☐ glue
☐ posterboard or cardboard
☐ pencils and erasers
☐ found objects*
☐ scissors ⚠S
☐ tempera or acrylic paints and paintbrushes

Studio 4: Draw to Show Space

☐ 12" × 18" drawing paper
☐ pencils
☐ colored pencils or water-based markers

Studio 5: Paint to Show Perspective

☐ 12" × 18" white paper
☐ rulers (optional)
☐ tempera paints and paintbrushes
☐ water-based markers

Studio 6: Show Value in a Monument Design

☐ 12" × 18" white drawing paper
☐ pencils
☐ black crayons, charcoal, felt-tip markers, or fine-lined pens

Studio 7: Experiment with Colors

☐ tempera or acrylic paints and paintbrushes
☐ mixing containers or trays
☐ 12" × 18" white paper
☐ pencils

Studio 8: Create Mood with Complementary Colors

☐ tempera or acrylic paints and paintbrushes
☐ pencils
☐ mixing containers or trays
☐ newsprint, 12" × 18" white paper

Studio 9: Make Textured Dinnerware

☐ newsprint
☐ pencils
☐ white glue
☐ heavy-duty paper plates, cups, or bowls*
☐ found objects such as beads, buttons, shells, and bottle caps*
☐ papier-mâché paste or wheat paste
☐ tempera paints and paintbrushes
☐ scissors ⚠S

Portfolio Project: Say It with Painted Flowers

☐ a vase with flowers
☐ white chalk
☐ oil pastels
☐ heavy black paper, newsprint

⚠S Educate students about safe use of these materials.

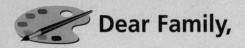 **Dear Family,**

In this unit, students will learn about the elements of art: line, shape, form, space, value, color, and texture. They will learn how these elements work together to make artworks expressive.

Students will study fine artworks, including those by Frida Kahlo, Vincent van Gogh, Fernand Léger, and Georgia O'Keeffe. A librarian or teacher can help you locate information about these artists to share with your child.

During this unit, your child will create artworks such as line drawings, a sculpted form, and a monument design. I invite you to display these artworks at home. I am gathering the materials we need to begin. If you would like to donate any of the following items, please send them in by the date of _____:

_____

_____

_____

_____

When your child brings home an artwork, ask questions such as the following:
- What elements of art did you use?
- What mood or feeling does your artwork express?
- How did the materials you chose affect your final creation?
- What techniques did you use to create the illusion of depth?

Thank you for experiencing art with your child!

Sincerely,

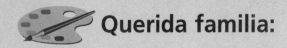 **Querida familia:**

En esta unidad los estudiantes aprenderán acerca de algunos elementos del arte como línea, figura, forma, espacio, valor, color y textura. Aprenderán también cómo estos elementos dan expresión a las obras de arte.

Estudiarán obras de arte, incluyendo obras de Frida Kahlo, Vincent van Gogh, Fernand Léger y Georgia O'Keeffe. Con ayuda de un(a) bibliotecario(a) o maestro(a) puede encontrar información sobre estos artistas para comentarla con su niño(a).

Durante el transcurso de esta unidad, su niño(a) también creará obras de arte, como dibujos lineales, formas esculpidas y el diseño de un monumento. Los invito a exhibir esos trabajos en el hogar. Estoy reuniendo los materiales que necesitamos para comenzar. Si usted deseara donar alguno de los siguientes artículos, por favor envíelos antes de la fecha _____:

_____

_____

_____

_____

Cuando su niño(a) traiga una de sus obras a casa, hágale preguntas como las siguientes:

- ¿Qué elementos de arte utilizaste?
- ¿Qué estado de ánimo o sentimiento expresas con tu arte?
- ¿Cómo influyeron los materiales que escogiste en tu obra terminada?
- ¿Qué técnicas usaste para dar sensación de profundidad?

¡Gracias por participar en la experiencia del arte con su niño(a)!

Atentamente,

Name _____

Vocabulary Practice 1

Draw a line from each word to its definition.

1. vertical lines

2. horizontal lines

3. geometric shapes

4. organic shapes

5. form

6. positive space

7. negative space

8. overlapping

9. linear perspective

10. vanishing point

A. a shape with three dimensions

B. creating illusion of space and depth on a two-dimensional surface with lines

C. lines that go up and down

D. the area around an object

E. irregular shapes like those found in nature

F. the point on the horizon where lines in a drawing come together

G. lines that are parallel to the horizon

H. an area occupied by an object

I. putting one object over another

J. precise, mathematical shapes like circles

Unit 1

☑ On the back of this paper, draw a design that shows geometric and organic shapes.

Práctica de vocabulario 1

Traza una línea desde cada palabra hasta su definición.

1. líneas verticales

2. líneas horizontales

3. figuras geométricas

4. figuras orgánicas

5. cuerpo

6. espacio positivo

7. espacio negativo

8. superponerse

9. perspectiva lineal

10. punto de fuga

A. figura con tres dimensiones

B. técnica con la cual, usando líneas, se crea la ilusión de espacio y profundidad en una superficie bidimensional

C. líneas que van de arriba a abajo

D. área alrededor de un objeto

E. figuras irregulares, como las que se encuentran en la naturaleza

F. punto en el horizonte donde convergen las líneas de un dibujo

G. obra de arte en tres dimensiones

H. ponerse un objeto delante o cubriendo a otro

I. líneas paralelas al horizonte

J. figuras matemáticas exactas, como los círculos

☑ Haz un dibujo en el que se vean figuras geométricas y orgánicas.

Name _____

Vocabulary Practice 2

Use each word or phrase in a sentence that relates to art or an artwork.

1. color scheme

_____

2. cross-hatching

_____

3. tactile texture

_____

4. monochromatic

_____

Draw a sketch that uses shading to show value. On the lines below your drawing, write a sentence that tells what shading technique you use to accomplish value.

5.

_____

_____

_____

☑ Turn the paper over. Write your first name in primary colors. Write your last name in secondary colors.

Práctica de vocabulario 2

Usa cada término en una oración relacionada con el arte o con una obra de arte.

1. conjunto de colores

_____

2. sombreado

_____

3. textura tactil

_____

4. monocromático

_____

Dibuja un boceto en el que apliques sombreado para mostrar diferentes valores. Luego escribe en las líneas de abajo una oración en la que expliques qué técnica de sombreado usaste para mostrar valores.

5.

_____

_____

_____

☑ En la parte de atrás de la hoja, escribe tu nombre con colores primarios y tu apellido con colores secundarios.

Name _____

Unit Test
Complete each sentence with a word or phrase from the Word Bank.

shading	sculpture	intermediate colors
depth	implied lines	

1. The lines between the two figures are _____ because they cannot clearly be seen.

2. It took the artist five years to carve the marble into a _____ in the shape of a lion.

3. The painter used _____ in perspective to make the circle in the painting seem to be a three-dimensional sphere.

4. In her portrait, the artist used _____ to show the shadows in the subject's face.

5. The artist used the _____ yellow-green and blue-green to create shadows on the trees in the background.

Draw something that shows two-point perspective.

6.

Name _____

Unit Test

Write a short paragraph that describes the difference between positive space and negative space. Give examples of each in your writing.

7. _____

_____

_____

_____

_____

_____

_____

Think about the artwork of Frida Kahlo, the artist featured in Look and Compare in Unit 1. Then use phrases or sentences to answer the following questions.

8. How does Kahlo create in her artwork a feeling of closeness and flat space without depth?

_____

_____

9. Why do you think Kahlo made some objects smaller and others larger in her paintings?

_____

_____

10. How did Kahlo create the illusion of depth and space in her paintings?

_____

_____

_____

Examen de la unidad

Completa cada oración con una palabra o frase del Banco de palabras.

sombreado	escultura	colores intermedios
profundidad	líneas implícitas	

1. Las líneas entre dos figuras son _____ porque no pueden verse a simple vista.

2. El artista tardó cinco años en tallar el mármol y crear una _____ de un león.

3. El pintor utilizó _____ en perspectiva para que el círculo de la pintura pareciera una esfera tridimensional.

4. En este retrato, la artista aplicó el _____ para mostrar las sombras en la cara de su modelo.

5. El artista utilizó los _____ verde-amarillo y verde-azul para crear sombras en los árboles del fondo.

Dibuja un esquema con perspectiva bifocal.

6.

Examen de la unidad

Escribe un párrafo corto en el que expliques la diferencia entre espacio positivo y espacio negativo. Da ejemplos de cada uno en tu explicación.

7. _____

_____

_____

_____

_____

_____

Piensa en la obra de Frida Kahlo, la artista que aparece en la sección "Mira y compara" de la Unidad 1. Luego responde a las preguntas con frases u oraciones.

8. ¿Cómo creó Kahlo una sensación de cercanía y espacio plano en su obra?

_____

_____

9. ¿Por qué crees que Kahlo hizo algunos de los objetos en su obra más pequeños y otros más grandes?

_____

_____

10. ¿Cómo logró Kahlo dar ilusión de profundidad y espacio en sus pinturas?

_____

_____

_____

Answer Key

Vocabulary Practice 1 & 2

Page 11

1. C	6. H
2. G	7. D
3. J	8. I
4. E	9. B
5. A	10. F

Page 13

1. Possible answer: The artist used a neutral color scheme of blacks, whites, and grays.
2. Possible answer: I can use cross-hatching to shade the figure's face.
3. Possible answer: The tactile texture of the alligator's skin feels bumpy.
4. Possible answer: Picasso used monochromatic shades of blue in many paintings.
5. Drawing should show light and dark contrast; sentence should describe shading technique.

Unit Test, Pages 15 and 16

1. implied lines
2. sculpture
3. depth
4. shading
5. intermediate colors
6. Students should draw two vanishing points to show space and depth on a two-dimensional surface.
7. Possible answer: Positive space is the area occupied by an object; negative space is the area around the object that defines its edges. Students could analyze the picture on page 28.
8. Kahlo uses repeated lines and large shapes next to other shapes instead of overlapping.
9. Kahlo creates perspective with this technique.
10. She created a foreground, middle ground, and background.

Práctica de vocabulario 1 y 2

Página 12

1. C	6. H
2. G	7. D
3. J	8. I
4. E	9. B
5. A	10. F

Página 14

1. Respuesta posible: El artista usó negro, blanco y gris para crear una gama de colores neutros.
2. Respuesta posible: Puedo usar el sombreado para cambiar la forma de una figura.
3. Respuesta posible: La textura tactil de la piel de un cocodrilo es húmeda.
4. Respuesta posible: Picasso usó variaciones monocromáticas de azul en muchas de sus pinturas.
5. Los bocetos deberán mostrar contraste de luz y sombra y las oraciones deberán describir la técnica del sombreado.

Examen de la unidad

Páginas 17 y 18

1. líneas implícitas
2. escultura
3. profundidad
4. sombreado
5. colores intermedios
6. Los estudiantes deben dibujar una perspectiva con dos puntos de fuga para dar sensación de espacio y profundidad en una superficie bidimensional.
7. Respuesta posible: Espacio positivo es el espacio ocupado por un objeto; espacio negativo es el área alrededor de un objeto que define sus bordes. Los estudiantes pueden analizar la ilustración de la página 28.
8. Kahlo utiliza repetidamente líneas y figuras grandes pegadas a otras figuras en lugar de superponerlas.
9. Con esta técnica Kahlo crea perspectiva.
10. La pintora creó un primer plano, un plano intermedio y un fondo.

Scoring Rubric

After each studio experience and the portfolio project, complete the following scoring rubric for each student.

Student Name:_____

- [ ] **Studio 1:** Gesture Drawing with Line
- [ ] **Studio 2:** Make a Tessellation
- [ ] **Studio 3:** Assemble a Form
- [ ] **Studio 4:** Draw to Show Space
- [ ] **Studio 5:** Paint to Show Perspective

- [ ] **Studio 6:** Show Value in a Monument Design
- [ ] **Studio 7:** Experiment with Colors
- [ ] **Studio 8:** Create Mood
- [ ] **Studio 9:** Make Textured Dinnerware
- [ ] **Portfolio Project:** Say It with Flowers

1 Poor	2 Fair	3 Good	4 Excellent
No instructions followed. No effort in problem solving. Shows no understanding of studio or project concept.	Some but not all instructions followed. Some effort in problem solving. Shows some understanding of studio or project concept.	All instructions followed. Basic use of problem-solving skills. Shows understanding of studio or project concept.	All instructions followed. Exceptional use of problem-solving skills. Shows notable creativity and originality in using the studio or project concept.

1 Insuficiente	2 Aceptable	3 Bueno	4 Excelente
No ha seguido las instrucciones. No se ha esforzado en resolver los problemas. No demuestra comprensión del concepto del taller o del proyecto.	Ha seguido algunas instrucciones, pero no todas. Demuestra algún esfuerzo en resolver los problemas. Demuestra alguna comprensión del concepto del taller o del proyecto.	Ha seguido todas las instrucciones. Demuestra un uso básico de destrezas de resolución de problemas. Demuestra comprensión del concepto del taller o del proyecto.	Ha seguido todas las instrucciones. Demuestra un uso excepcional de destrezas de resolución de problemas. Demuestra destacada creatividad y originalidad al aplicar el concepto del taller o del proyecto.

Unit 1 Self-Check

Unit Concepts

1. The elements of art that I find most interesting in artworks of others are _____

   _____ because _____

   _____

   _____

2. I will most likely use the elements of _____

   in my own artwork because _____

   _____

   _____

Studios and Portfolio Project

3. Which studio/project was the most difficult? Why?

   _____

4. What would you do differently next time?

   _____

5. Which studio/project was the most creative for expressing your ideas?

   _____

6. What unit concepts helped you with the studios/project?

   _____

7. What did you learn from creating the artworks in this unit?

   _____

8. What technique would you like to explore further?

   _____

Unidad 1 Autoevaluación

Conceptos de la unidad

1. Los elementos de arte que me resultan más interesantes en las obras de otros son

_____ porque _____

_____

_____

2. Lo más probable es que yo use los elementos del _____

en mis propias obras porque _____

_____

_____

Talleres y proyecto para el portafolio

3. ¿Qué taller o proyecto fue el más difícil? ¿Por qué?

_____

4. ¿Qué harías de manera diferente la próxima vez?

_____

5. ¿Qué taller o proyecto te permitió expresar tus ideas de manera más creativa? ¿Por qué?

_____

6. ¿Qué conceptos aprendidos en esta unidad te sirvieron de ayuda para realizar los talleres o el proyecto?

_____

7. ¿Qué aprendiste al crear tus obras de arte en esta unidad?

_____

8. ¿Qué técnica te gustaría explorar más?

_____

Curriculum Connection

Music

Materials

- ☐ tape recorder
- ☐ writing paper, pens or pencils
- ☐ p. 17 of Student Edition

Research Van Gogh's Life Have students work in small groups to research Vincent van Gogh's life. Have group members work together to write a song based on the painting *The Starry Night* and the artist's life. Have students tape record the song and play the tape for the class. Then have students explain the ways in which the song lyrics reflect both the elements of the painting as well as aspects of Van Gogh's life.

Technology

Materials

- ☐ computer
- ☐ printer and paper
- ☐ graphic arts software

Computer Tessellations Have pairs of students work together to create a computer tessellation that includes a variety of geometric and/or organic shapes. Encourage them to experiment with colors to give their tessellation greater depth. After students print their designs, have partners switch papers to identify the shapes and the effect of color.

Science

Materials

- ☐ magazines
- ☐ glue
- ☐ scissors ⚠
- ☐ 12" × 18" white drawing paper

Forms in Nature Collage Have students work independently to make a collage showing some of the forms found in nature. Students can depict geometric and organic forms by cutting magazine pictures apart or using them as they appear. Display the collages and have the class identify the forms.

Visual Culture

Materials

- ☐ newspaper and magazine ads
- ☐ empty product containers
- ☐ writing paper, pens or pencils

Analyze Color in Words One at a time, display each of the ads or containers and have the class analyze the effect of color and value. For example, ask students why steel wool pads might be packaged in a bold red box but baby shampoo in a soft yellow container. Then have students choose one ad or container and write a paragraph explaining how the colors, their values, and the color scheme affect our perception of the item.

Culminating Activities

Museum Project: Exploring the Elements of Art

Take students to an art museum or on a virtual tour to analyze the elements of art such as line, shape, form, and color. For virtual tours, see a Web site such as The Metropolitan Museum of Art (www.metmuseum.org). Remember to guide students in using safe Internet practices. Ⓢ

Before You Go

Review the elements of art that students learned in this unit. Then explain to students that when they visit art museums, they should use what they learned to analyze the works of art they see. Tell the class that they will visit a real or a virtual museum to find appealing artworks and use what they know to further their appreciation and understanding of the artists' mastery.

During the Visit

Review the elements of art while on the tour.

- Have each student locate an artwork that exemplifies one or more of the art elements, study the artwork to find the element, and explain how the artist uses it to create a mood or effect.
- Have students draw the artwork in their Sketchbook Journals and write a caption that explains how the element creates the feeling. Students should also note why they selected this specific element of art.

When You Return

Have students create their own museum by arranging their drawings and captions in the classroom.

Performing Arts: Tableau Vivant

After completing Studio 8 on page 51, have students use music and dance to create a mood with complementary colors.

Prepare

Arrange students in small groups. Have each group follow these steps:

- Choose a palette of complementary colors. Assign one pair of complementary colors to each group member. Students should not reveal the colors to the rest of the class.
- Create a dance that captures the mood of the complementary colors.
- Choose music that reinforces the mood created by the colors.

Practice

Allow each group sufficient time to practice their dance. Remind students to keep their color scheme secret.

Perform

Have each group perform its dance to the background music they have selected while the rest of the class analyzes the mood to guess the complementary colors being expressed. During the question-and-answer period, have each group reveal their color choices, explain what mood they expressed, and tell why.

Overview

Many prominent artists are featured in Unit 2, such as:

Georges Braque
Cubist painter

Georges Braque. *The Round Table*, 1929. Oil on canvas, 57 by 44 inches. The Phillips Collection, Washington, D.C.

Unit Contents

Materials List 26
Family Letter 27
Vocabulary Practice 1 29
Vocabulary Practice 2 31
Unit Test 33
Answer Key 37
Scoring Rubric 38
Self-Check 39
Curriculum Connection 41
Curriculum Activities 42

Unit Vocabulary

1. principles of design, balance, symmetrical balance, asymmetrical balance, radial balance
2. emphasis
3. proportion, standard proportion, altered proportion
4. rhythm, regular rhythm, alternating rhythm, progressive rhythm
5. pattern, Cubism
6. unity
7. variety

Unit 2

Materials List

Below are materials needed for each studio experience and the portfolio project. Materials followed by an* are items families might be able to donate.

Studio 1: Make a Pendant

- [ ] sheets of 8½" × 11" colored wallpaper
- [ ] felt-tip pens
- [ ] rulers
- [ ] glue
- [ ] scissors ⚠
- [ ] cotton swabs
- [ ] fishing line or string
- [ ] wire
- [ ] needle-nose pliers ⚠

Studio 2: Emphasize to Show Meaning

- [ ] pencils and felt-tip pens
- [ ] scissors ⚠
- [ ] 2 sheets of dark-colored construction paper per student
- [ ] 12" × 18" sheets of white paper
- [ ] glue
- [ ] various types and colors of paper, such as wrapping, tissue, metallic*

Studio 3: Design a Sculpture

- [ ] magazines or a camera
- [ ] pencils with soft lead, pens, or felt-tip markers
- [ ] white drawing paper
- [ ] paper for photocopying

Studio 4: Create Rhythmic Shapes

- [ ] variety of colored construction paper
- [ ] 12" × 18" white paper
- [ ] glue
- [ ] colored pencils

Studio 5: Make a Patterned Clay Pot

- [ ] plastic mat to cover the table
- [ ] lumps of wedged clay
- [ ] implements you can use to make patterns, such as plastic forks, pencils, or interesting drawer pulls*
- [ ] slip
- [ ] clay glazes or watercolors, paintbrushes

Studio 6: Assemble a Unified Composition

- [ ] wood scraps and shapes*
- [ ] tempera paints, paintbrushes
- [ ] mixing trays or plates
- [ ] wood glue
- [ ] water containers*
- [ ] medium binder clips
- [ ] small, sturdy cardboard boxes of different sizes, none larger than a shoebox, 3 per student*

Studio 7: Make a Fabric Hanging

- [ ] variety of patterned fabrics*
- [ ] large pieces of fabric, approximately 18" × 22"
- [ ] scissors ⚠
- [ ] glue
- [ ] small tree branches or dowels*
- [ ] raffia, twine, rope, or strips of fabric*

Portfolio Project: Homescape

- [ ] neighborhood sketches from Sketchbook Journal activity (optional)
- [ ] 11" × 17" heavy drawing paper and newsprint
- [ ] tempera paints and paintbrushes
- [ ] mixing trays or plates and water containers*
- [ ] pencils
- [ ] black or colored markers

⚠ Educate students about safe use of these materials.

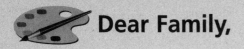 **Dear Family,**

In this unit, students will learn about the principles of design, including balance, emphasis, proportion, rhythm, pattern, unity, and variety. They will learn how these principles can help an artist express a particular idea.

Fine artworks, including those by Georges Braque, Marc Chagall, José Cuneo, and Sonia Terk Delaunay, will be studied. A librarian or teacher can help you locate information about these artists to share with your child.

During this unit, your child will create artworks such as a pendant, a patterned clay box, and a fabric hanging. I invite you to display these artworks at home. I am gathering the materials we need to begin. If you would like to donate any of the following items, please send them in by the date of _____:

_____

_____

_____

_____

When your child brings home an artwork, ask questions such as the following:
- What area of the composition did you emphasize?
- How did you use proportion in your composition and what effect does it have?
- Which of your artworks do you like the most? Why?

Thank you for experiencing art with your child!

Sincerely,

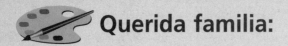 **Querida familia:**

En esta unidad los estudiantes aprenderán los principios del diseño, incluyendo equilibrio, énfasis, proporción, ritmo, patrón, unidad y variedad. Aprenderán de qué manera estos principios facilitan al artista la expresión de una idea determinada.

Se estudiarán obras de arte, incluyendo las de Georges Braque, Marc Chagall, José Cuneo y Sonia Terk Delaunay. Si necesita información sobre alguno de estos artistas, pídasela a un(a) bibliotecario(a) o a un(a) maestro(a).

Durante el transcurso de esta unidad, su niño(a) también creará obras de arte, como un pendiente, una caja de arcilla con un patrón decorativo y una tela colgante. Los invito a exhibir esos trabajos en el hogar. Estoy reuniendo los materiales que necesitamos para comenzar. Si usted deseara donar alguno de los siguientes artículos, por favor envíelos antes de la fecha _____:

_____

_____

_____

_____

Cuando su niño(a) traiga sus trabajos a casa, hágale preguntas como las siguientes:

- ¿En qué área de la composición hiciste énfasis?
- ¿Cómo aplicaste la proporción en tu composición y qué efecto tuvo?
- ¿Cuál de tus obras es tu preferida? ¿Por qué?

¡Gracias por participar en la experiencia del arte con su niño(a)!

Atentamente,

Name _____

Vocabulary Practice 1

Use each word or phrase in a sentence that relates to art or an artwork.

1. balance

_____

2. emphasis

_____

3. proportion

_____

4. altered proportion

_____

5. radial balance

_____

Draw a sketch that shows symmetrical balance and asymmetrical balance. On the lines below your sketch, write a sentence that explains how you created each type of balance.

6.

_____

_____

☑ Turn page over. Use all five vocabulary words from this page in one sentence.

Práctica de vocabulario 1

Usa cada palabra en una oración relacionada con el arte o con una obra de arte.

1. equilibrio

_____

2. énfasis

_____

3. proporciones

_____

4. proporciones alteradas

_____

5. equilibrio radial

_____

Dibuja un esquema en el que se vea equilibrio simétrico y asimétrico. En las líneas de abajo, escribe una oración para explicar cómo creaste cada tipo de equilibrio.

6.

_____

_____

 En la parte de atrás de la hoja, escribe una oración en la que uses las cinco palabras de vocabulario de esta página.

Name _____

Vocabulary Practice 2

Complete the crossword puzzle with vocabulary words from Lessons 4 to 7.

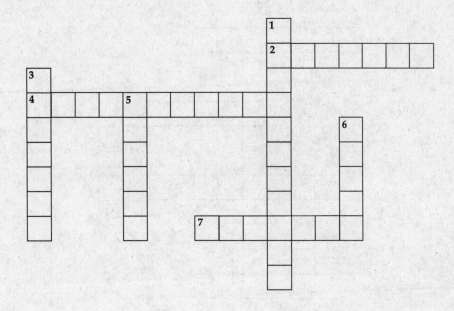

Across

2. a type of rhythm in art that involves the repetition of an element without variation

4. a type of rhythm in art that involves the repetition of two or more elements in an even pattern

7. the use of different elements to add interest to an artwork

Down

1. a type of rhythm that shows regular changes in a repeated element

3. repeated colors, lines, shapes, or forms in an artwork

5. the repetition of visual elements that creates a feeling of motion in an artwork

6. the quality of seeming whole

 On the back of this page, use the same words to make a different type of puzzle.

Práctica de vocabulario 2

Completa el crucigrama con palabras del vocabulario de las Lecciones 4 a 7.

Horizontales

2. en arte, tipo de ritmo creado por la repetición uniforme de dos o más elementos que se intercalan

3. en arte, tipo de ritmo creado por la repetición de un mismo elemento sin variaciones

6. uso de elementos diferentes para dar más interés a una obra de arte

7. calidad de uno, entero

Verticales

1. ritmo dado por elementos que se repiten y van cambiando continuamente de manera regular

4. repetición de elementos visuales en una obra de arte, que produce una sensación de movimiento

5. en una obra de arte, los colores, líneas, figuras y formas que se repiten pueden formar un

 En la parte de atrás de la hoja, haz otro tipo de ejercicio con estas mismas palabras.

Unit 2

Name _____

Unit Test

Complete each sentence with a vocabulary word or phrase from Unit 2.

1. The artist uses pattern and color to achieve _____ in the composition so that it is complete and harmonious.

2. You can create _____ in a picture by stressing a specific feature, such as a tree or building.

3. A bicycle wheel has _____ because the spokes of the wheel spread out in a regular pattern from a central point.

4. The fabric has a pretty _____ of repeated colors and shapes.

5. The composition has _____ because the figure seems to have appropriate height, width, and depth.

Draw a scene that has a pattern.

6.

Unit 2

Unit Test

Complete the following analogy.

7. *Proportion* is to *balance* as *altered proportion* is to _____ .

    a. pattern   c. asymmetrical balance

    b. symmetrical balance   d. rhythm

Explain your response.

_____

_____

_____

_____

Think about the art of Braque and Lentulov, the artists featured in Look and Compare in Unit 2. In the space provided, write **T** if the statement is true or **F** if the statement is false.

_____ 8. Braque and Lentulov rejected the paintings of the French artist Paul Cézanne, especially his use of balance and variety.

_____ 9. Lentulov copied the Cubist style exactly because he liked the soft, colorful paintings of that movement.

_____ 10. Both artists broke down form into colored shapes to create patterns.

Examen de la unidad

Completa cada oración con una palabra o frase de la Unidad 2.

1. El artista utiliza un patrón y colores para lograr dar _____ a la composición, de modo que ésta resulte completa y armoniosa.

2. Puedes dar _____ a parte de una ilustración destacando una parte específica de ella, por ejemplo, un árbol o una construcción.

3. La rueda de una bicicleta tiene _____ porque los rayos se distribuyen en un patrón regular saliendo todos del mismo punto central.

4. La tela tiene un hermoso _____ de colores y figuras que se repiten.

5. La composición tiene _____ porque la figura parece tener la altura, el ancho y la profundidad apropiadas y naturales.

Dibuja una escena que contenga un patrón.

6.

Examen de la unidad

Completa la siguiente analogía.

7. *La proporción es al equilibrio lo que las proporciones alteradas son al* _____.

    a. patrón   b. equilibrio asimétrico

    c. equilibrio simétrico   c. ritmo

Explica tu respuesta.

_____

_____

_____

_____

Piensa en el arte de Braque y Lentulov, los artistas que aparecen en la sección "Mira y compara" de la Unidad 2. En el espacio en blanco junto a cada oración, escribe **V** si la oración es verdadera y **F** si es falsa.

_____ **8.** Braque y Lentulov no aprobaban las pinturas del artista francés Paul Cézanne, especialmente su uso del equilibrio y la variedad.

_____ **9.** Lentulov copió el estilo cubista exactamente porque le gustaban las pinturas coloridas y suaves características de este movimiento.

_____ **10.** Ambos artistas descomponían las formas en figuras coloridas para crear patrones.

Answer Key

Vocabulary Practice 1 & 2

Page 29

1. Possible answer: The artist created balance by arranging parts to create a sense that the visual weight is equal overall.

2. Possible answer: The painter drew our attention to the key element in the picture by using emphasis.

3. Possible answer: The picture had a pleasant proportion because the parts were linked.

4. Possible answer: The figure's elongated arms and legs showed altered proportion.

5. *South Rose Window* shows radial balance.

6. Students should explain that they achieved symmetrical balance by matching both sides and asymmetrical balance by having both sides carry similar visual weight, although they are not identical.

Page 31

Across	Down
2. regular	1. progressive
4. alternating	3. pattern
7. variety	5. rhythm
	6. unity

Unit Test, Pages 33 and 34

1. unity
2. emphasis
3. radial balance
4. pattern
5. standard proportion

6. Students should show a scene that has repeated lines, shapes, forms, or textures.

7. C. Proportion and balance both describe symmetry, while altered proportion and asymmetrical balance both describe the absence of uniformity.

8. F
9. F
10. T

Práctica de vocabulario 1 y 2

Página 30

1. Respuesta posible: El artista creó equilibrio acomodando las partes de modo que den la sensación de que todas tienen igual importancia visual en el conjunto.

2. Respuesta posible: El pintor dirigió nuestra atención al elemento principal del cuadro dándole *énfasis*.

3. Respuesta posible: La pintura tenía proporciones agradables porque sus partes estaban relacionadas.

4. Respuesta posible: Los brazos y las piernas alargados de la figura dejan ver que se han usado proporciones alteradas.

5. *South Rose Window* muestra equilibrio radial.

6. Los estudiantes deben explicar que lograron equilibrio simétrico al emparejar ambos lados y equilibrio asimétrico al dar a ambos lados la misma importancia visual, aunque no sean idénticos.

Página 32

Horizontales	Verticales
2. alterno	1. progresivo
3. regular	4. ritmo
6. variedad	5. patrón
7. unidad	

Examen de la unidad, Páginas 35 y 36

1. unidad
2. énfasis
3. equilibrio radial
4. patrón
5. proporciones naturales

6. Los estudiantes deben dibujar una escena en la que haya un patrón de líneas, figuras, formas o colores que se repitan.

7. C. La proporción y el equilibrio son características de la simetría, mientras que las proporciones alteradas y el equilibrio asimétrico son características de la falta de uniformidad.

8. F
9. F
10. V

Scoring Rubric

After each studio experience and the portfolio project, complete the following scoring rubric for each student.

Student Name:_____

☐ **Studio 1:** Make a Pendant   ☐ **Studio 5:** Make a Patterned Clay Pot

☐ **Studio 2:** Emphasize to Show Meaning   ☐ **Studio 6:** Assemble a Unified Composition

☐ **Studio 3:** Design a Sculpture   ☐ **Studio 7:** Make a Fabric Hanging

☐ **Studio 4:** Create Rhythmic Shapes   ☐ **Portfolio Project:** Homescape

1 Poor	2 Fair	3 Good	4 Excellent
No instructions followed. No effort in problem solving. Shows no understanding of studio or project concept.	Some but not all instructions followed. Some effort in problem solving. Shows some understanding of studio or project concept.	All instructions followed. Basic use of problem-solving skills. Shows understanding of studio or project concept.	All instructions followed. Exceptional use of problem-solving skills. Shows notable creativity and originality in using the studio or project concept.

1 Insuficiente	2 Aceptable	3 Bueno	4 Excelente
No ha seguido las instrucciones. No se ha esforzado en resolver los problemas. No demuestra comprensión del concepto del taller o del proyecto.	Ha seguido algunas instrucciones, pero no todas. Demuestra algún esfuerzo en resolver los problemas. Demuestra alguna comprensión del concepto del taller o del proyecto.	Ha seguido todas las instrucciones. Demuestra un uso básico de destrezas de resolución de problemas. Demuestra comprensión del concepto del taller o del proyecto.	Ha seguido todas las instrucciones. Demuestra un uso excepcional de destrezas de resolución de problemas. Demuestra destacada creatividad y originalidad al aplicar el concepto del taller o del proyecto.

Unit 2 Self-Check

Unit Concepts

1. I think the most important principles of design are _____

   because _____

   _____

2. The design principles that I would like to learn more about are _____

   because _____

   _____

Studios and Portfolio Project

3. Which studio/project was the most difficult? Why?

   _____

4. What would you do differently next time?

   _____

5. Which studio/project was the most creative for expressing your ideas?

   _____

6. What unit concepts helped you with the studios/project?

   _____

7. What did you learn from creating the artworks in this unit?

   _____

8. What technique would you like to explore further?

   _____

Unidad 2 Autoevaluación

Conceptos de la unidad

1. Pienso que los principios más importantes del diseño son _____

   porque _____

   _____

2. Los principios del diseño que me gustaría aprender mejor son _____

   porque _____

   _____

Talleres y proyecto para el portafolio

3. ¿Qué taller o proyecto fue el más difícil? ¿Por qué?

   _____

4. ¿Qué harías de manera diferente la próxima vez?

   _____

5. ¿Qué taller o proyecto te permitió expresar tus ideas de manera más creativa? ¿Por qué?

   _____

6. ¿Qué conceptos aprendidos en esta unidad te sirvieron de ayuda para realizar los talleres o el proyecto?

   _____

7. ¿Qué aprendiste al crear tus obras de arte en esta unidad?

   _____

8. ¿Qué técnica te gustaría explorar más?

   _____

Curriculum Connection

Language Arts

Materials

☐ dictionaries
☐ writing paper, pens or pencils

Palindromes Tell students that palindromes are words, phrases, or sentences that read the same backwards or forwards, such as eye, racecar, and Madam, I'm Adam. Explain that palindromes show symmetrical balance since both sides are the same. Have groups of students find and list other palindromes and share them with the class.

Social Studies

Materials

☐ political cartoons
☐ history books
☐ computers with Internet access

Research Political Cartoons Partner students to locate a contemporary or historical political cartoon in a history book or online. Then have partners analyze the cartoon's meaning and use of emphasis. Last, have partners display the cartoon and describe how the artist created emphasis through exaggeration or contrast. Remember to guide students in using safe Internet practices. Ⓢ

Physical Education

Materials

☐ music on CD or tapes
☐ CD player or tape recorder

Rhythm in Motion Have students work in small groups to create a series of exercises or dances that show rhythm through motion and the repetition of visual elements. The rhythm can be random or regular, alternating or progressive. After each group performs, have the rest of the class identify the types of rhythm they saw.

Math

Materials

☐ writing paper
☐ pens or pencils

Fibonacci and Friends Write the following Fibonacci pattern on the chalkboard: 0, 1, 1, 2, 3, 5, 8. Challenge the class to find the next number (13) and explain how they derived it (each number in the pattern is the sum of the previous two digits). Have individual students work to create logical patterns with numbers. Have students swap patterns, solve for the next number, and explain how they derived it.

Culminating Activities

Museum Project: Studying Design

Take students to an art museum or on a virtual tour to analyze the principles of design such as balance, proportion, pattern, and variety. For virtual tours, see a Web site such as The Cleveland Museum of Art (**www.clemusart.org**). Remember to guide students in using safe Internet practices. ⚠ⓢ

Before You Go

Remind students of what they learned in the Unit 1 Museum Project. Then discuss with the class how they should use what they learned about the principles of design as they study what they see. Explain to the class that they will visit a real or virtual museum to find well-known works of art.

During the Visit

Review the principles of design while on the tour.

- Have students locate an artwork that demonstrates one or more of the principles of design. Direct students to study the artwork to discover what makes it celebrated.
- In their Sketchbook Journals, have students create their own variation by drawing the artwork but varying one of the principles of design.

When You Return

Have students display their drawings and explain what they varied and why, and the effect it had on the artwork.

Performing Arts: Improvisational Skit

After completing Lesson 5 on page 80, have students create skits showing how the pattern in a typical school day can vary, depending on the decisions and events of the day.

Prepare

Form small groups. Have the first group write a brief skit portraying an average day in school. The skit should:
- Show three-to-four commonplace events
- Have simple dialogue and actions
- Take about three minutes to perform

Practice

Allow the first group sufficient time to practice its skit.

Perform

Have the first group perform its skit. Then have each group in turn copy the skit but make one minor variation. For instance, they might change the last event slightly or vary the dialogue. Each group must exactly copy the previous skit but add one variation. At the end of all improvs, discuss the resulting pattern.

Overview

Many prominent artists are featured in Unit 3, such as:

Louise Nelson

Contemporary sculptor

Louise Nevelson. *Atmosphere and Environment V,* 1966. Enamel on aluminum, 96 by 102 by 324 inches. Corning Tower Plaza, Albany, NY.

Unit Contents

Materials List 44
Family Letter 45
Vocabulary Practice 1 47
Vocabulary Practice 2 49
Unit Test 51
Answer Key 55
Scoring Rubric 56
Self-Check 57
Curriculum Connection 59
Culminating Activities 60

Unit Vocabulary

1. art media, techniques, medium, light source, subject

2. oil-based paint, water-based paints, tempera paint, palette, transparent, opaque, automatic drawing

3. block, plate, printmaking, relief print, intaglio print, lithograph

4. collage, mixed media

5. weaving, textiles, fiber arts, stitchery, quilt, triptych

6. assembling, casting, armature, relief sculpture, symbols

7. architect, architecture, elevation, blueprints, landscape architecture

8. pottery, applied art, decorative art, ceramics, slip, glazes

9. still photography, video art

10. digital technology, computer art, software, scanner, Web design

Materials List

Below are materials needed for each studio experience and the portfolio project. Materials followed by an * are items families might be able to donate.

Studio 1: Show Light

- ☐ sections of white plastic pipe
- ☐ newsprint, heavy white drawing paper
- ☐ charcoal, oil pastels
- ☐ lamps or other strong light sources

Studio 2: Combine Tempera with Other Media

- ☐ watercolor paper, tissue paper*
- ☐ tempera paints and paintbrushes
- ☐ India ink and paintbrushes, chalk

Studio 3: Print in Combinations

- ☐ unused square pink erasers
- ☐ tempera paints
- ☐ 8" × 12" heavy drawing paper
- ☐ 6" × 10" linoleum blocks
- ☐ linoleum cutters ⚠
- ☐ brayers and printing ink
- ☐ inking plates or clean plastic foam meat trays*
- ☐ spoons*

Studio 4: Make a Collage with Dimension

- ☐ glue, scissors ⚠
- ☐ foam core or posterboard
- ☐ railroad board or tagboard
- ☐ cloth, paper, and found objects*
- ☐ water-based markers and paint

Studio 5: Make a Mixed-Media Triptych

- ☐ newsprint, pencils
- ☐ fabric and felt in many colors*
- ☐ 8" × 15" rectangles of fabric, 3 per student*
- ☐ fabric glue, scissors ⚠
- ☐ acrylic paints and paintbrushes

Studio 6: Create Symbols in Bas-Relief

- ☐ low-fire clay and slip
- ☐ rolling pins, carving tools ⚠
- ☐ plastic wrap*
- ☐ glazes and paintbrushes

Studio 7: Design a Public Landscape

- ☐ graph paper
- ☐ cardboard templates (optional)
- ☐ colored pencils, pencils, rulers

Studio 8: Create a Textured Ceramic Jar

- ☐ low-fire clay and slip
- ☐ items to score and scratch in texture*

Studio 9: Colorize a Photograph

- ☐ personal photographs from family collections or new photographs*
- ☐ camera and scanner (optional)
- ☐ photocopier or computer printer
- ☐ black-and-white versions of the photographs
- ☐ colored pencils, watercolors, or computer software

Studio 10: Design a Web Page

- ☐ graph paper
- ☐ pencils, pens, and markers
- ☐ computer and Web page design program (optional)

Portfolio Project: Make a Multimedia Sculpture

- ☐ wood, such as tree limbs or 2" × 4"s*
- ☐ wire, nails, or screws* ⚠
- ☐ glue and masking tape
- ☐ newspapers*
- ☐ papier-mâché strips and paste
- ☐ pieces of cloth, paper, and found objects*
- ☐ acrylic paints, varnish, and paintbrushes

⚠ Educate students about safe use of these materials.

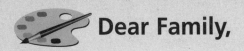 **Dear Family,**

In this unit, students will learn about art media and techniques, including painting with different kinds of paint, printmaking, weaving, still photography, video art, and computer art. They will learn how these different media and techniques help artists express themselves.

Students will study fine artworks, including those by Robert McIntosh, Robin Shepherd, Jaune Quick-to-See Smith, and Louise Nevelson. A librarian or teacher can help you locate information about these artists.

During this unit, your child will create artworks such as a mixed-media triptych, a bas-relief, and a textured ceramic jar. I invite you to display these artworks at home. I am gathering the materials we need to begin. If you would like to donate any of the following items, please send them in by the date of _____:

_____

_____

_____

_____

When your child brings home an artwork, ask questions such as the following:
- What art media did you use in this artwork? How do you think your choice of medium affected the artwork?
- What technique or techniques did you use? Why?
- What was the most challenging part of creating this artwork?

Thank you for experiencing art with your child!

Sincerely,

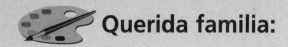

Querida familia:

En esta unidad, los estudiantes aprenderán sobre los materiales y las técnicas de arte, incluyendo pintura con diferentes tipos de pinturas, grabados, tejidos, fotografía, video y arte computarizado. Aprenderán de qué manera estos diferentes medios y técnicas permiten a los artistas lograr resultados especiales y expresar sus ideas.

Los estudiantes examinarán obras de arte, incluyendo las de Robert McIntosh, Robin Shepherd, Jaune Quick-to-See Smith y Louise Nevelson. Un(a) bibliotecario(a) o maestro(a) puede ayudarle e encontrar información sobre estos artistas.

Durante el transcurso de esta unidad, su niño(a) también creará obras de arte, como un tríptico de materiales mixtos, un bajorrelieve y un jarrón de cerámica texturizada. Invito a la familia a exhibir esos trabajos en el hogar. Estoy reuniendo los materiales que necesitamos para comenzar. Si usted deseara donar alguno de los siguientes artículos, por favor envíelos antes de la fecha _____:

_____

_____

_____

_____

Cuando su niño(a) traiga sus trabajos a casa, hágale preguntas como las siguientes:

- ¿Qué medios de arte utilizaste en esta obra? ¿Cómo crees que influyeron los medios o materiales que escogiste en el resultado de tu obra?
- ¿Qué técnica o técnicas utilizaste? ¿Por qué?
- ¿Qué fue lo más difícil al crear esta obra? Explica tu respuesta.

¡Gracias por participar en la experiencia del arte con su niño(a)!

Atentamente,

Vocabulary Practice 1

Complete each sentence with a word from the Word Bank. Then use the letters in the boxes to answer the question.

> block   collage   stitchery   lithograph   palette
> textiles   medium   weaving   plate

1. The material that an artist uses to create an artwork is called the
   □ __ __ __ __ __.

2. Paints can be mixed on a flat surface called a __ __ __ __ □ __ __.

3. A design is carved into a wood or linoleum __ __ __ __ □ for printing.

4. An intaglio print is scratched into a thin sheet of metal called a □ __ __ __ __.

5. A __ __ __ __ __ __ __ __ □ __ __ is a method of printing from a flat stone.

6. A __ __ __ __ __ □ __ is a design made by attaching a variety of materials to a flat surface.

7. An ancient technique of interlacing fibers or yarn is __ __ __ __ __ □ __.

8. Artworks or fabrics made of yarn or fibers are __ __ __ __ □ __ __ __.

9. A form of fiber art used to add decoration to cloth is
   __ __ __ __ __ __ __ □ __.

Question: What is the process by which multiple copies of an image can be made?

Answer: __ __ __ __ __ __ __ __ __ __ __
       4   9   8   7   2   1   5   3   8   7   6

☑ Turn the paper over. Name three different types of paint and explain how they are alike and how they are different.

Práctica de vocabulario 1

Completa cada oración con una palabra del Banco de palabras. Luego usa las letras que queden dentro de los recuadros para completar la respuesta de la Pregunta 10.

bloque	collage	costura	litografía	paleta
medio	tejido	placa	textiles	

1. El material que un artista utiliza para crear una obra también es llamado
   ▢ __ __ __ __ .

2. Las pinturas se pueden mezclar en una superficie plana llamada la
   __ __ __ ▢ __ __ del pintor.

3. Un diseño tallado en un ▢ __ __ __ __ __ de linóleo.

4. Un grabado en intaglio se raya sobre una lámina de metal llamada
   ▢ __ __ __ __ de grabado.

5. Una __ __ __ __ __ ▢ __ __ __ __ se obtiene por un método que consiste
   en imprimir a partir de una piedra plana.

6. Un __ __ __ __ __ ▢ __ es un diseño obtenido al pegar variados materiales
   sobre una superficie plana.

7. El __ __ __ __ __ ▢ es una técnica antiquísima que consiste en entrelazar
   fibras o lanas.

8. Los __ __ __ __ ▢ __ __ __ son telas hechas de hilos o fibras.

9. La __ __ ▢ __ __ __ __ y el bordado son tipos de arte con fibras usados para
   decorar una tela.

Pregunta: ¿Cuál es el nombre de un proceso con el que se pueden hacer múltiples copias
de una misma imagen?

Respuesta: __ __ __ r __ __ __ __ n   de   __ ra __ ados
          8 1 4   2 9 5 7   6   3

✔ En la parte de atrás de la hoja, escribe tres diferentes tipos de pinturas y explica en
qué se parecen y en qué se diferencian.

Vocabulary Practice 2

Read the clues. Circle the words in the puzzle.

```
A R M I T U R E S E Y C
S R I S C A N N E R W A
S E C T O R T H E E A S
E T H H S F O T R N R T
M B C B I W T M Y O H I
B R L E N T Y W T I O N
L A A A T R E C A R L G
I N N Q E I N C N R N Y
N D G T T S H R T L E A
G T T O N E L C R U O A
O O P S E S E S R F R R
P R O A T G E T P A S E
```

Diagonal

1. artist who designs buildings
2. building design
3. functional art made of clay
4. computer applications

Across

5. wire model over clay
6. device that transfers visuals to computer

Down

7. putting together
8. molding technique for sculpture

 Choose four of the words in the puzzle, and on the back of this page draw a picture to illustrate them.

Práctica de vocabulario 2

Lee las definiciones, encuentra cada una de las palabras en la sopa de letras y enciérrala en un círculo.

Unit 3

```
A B C D E F G H I J K L M E N O
P R Q L L A G E Q R I S R N A L
A R Q U I T E C T U R A A S I T
B A T U K S I D E L W Y M A I C
C H E L I S E Q U T I E R M E N
M E U C H T O E F I T L U B E M
X I R X O L E O C S T L T L C O
R O D A L E S C A N E R T A S L
C E R A M I C H T E L O E R R D
I L E H C I I M R O S I C A M E
S T A H E G C A B A D O T J B A
K M T R L M R A I M A S O H O R
```

Diagonales

1. artista que diseña edificios y casas
2. alfarería de arcilla cocida
3. programas de computación

Horizontales

4. arte y ciencia de planear construcciones
5. aparato que transfiere elementos visuales a una computadora

Verticales

6. poner juntas las piezas de una obra o instalación
7. hacer una escultura con la técnica de verter material fundido en un molde

 Escoge cuatro de las palabras del rompecabezas e ilústralas en la parte de atrás de la hoja.

Unit Test

Draw a line from each word to its definition.

1. oil-based paint

2. mixed media

3. fiber art

4. still photography

5. computer art

A. art created with the help of software and scanners

B. images captured on light-sensitive paper

C. paint that uses linseed oil as the binder

D. weaving

E. artwork that combines materials, such as paint or ink as well as collage

Draw an artist creating an artwork using one of the techniques from Unit 3.
Label your drawing.

6.

Unit 3

Unit 3

Unit Test

Explain the difference between applied art and decorative art. Tell when you would use each one.

7. _____

_____

_____

_____

_____

_____

_____

Think about Kurt Schwitters' artwork, as described in Look and Compare in Unit 3. Answer each question in a complete sentence.

8. What feature distinguishes Schwitters' style?

_____

_____

9. How did Schwitters use the word *Merz* to describe his artwork?

_____

_____

10. How are the artworks of Schwitters and Nevelson alike?

_____

_____

Examen de la unidad

Traza una línea de cada palabra a su definición.

1. pintura al óleo

2. materiales mixtos

3. arte textil

4. fotografía fija

5. arte computarizado

A. arte creado mediante el uso de computadoras

B. imágenes capturadas en papel fotosensible

C. pintura que tiene aceite de linaza como base

D. tejido

E. obra de arte hecha con pintura o tinta y, a la vez, collage

Haz un esquema de un artista creando una obra con una de las técnicas de la Unidad 3. Pon título a tu dibujo.

6.

Nombre _____

Examen de la unidad

Explica la diferencia entre arte aplicado y decorativo. Indica en qué casos usarías cada uno.

7. _____

_____

_____

_____

_____

_____

_____

_____

Piensa en cómo Kurt Schwitters hizo obras de arte a partir de objetos de uso cotidiano, como se describe en la sección Mira y compara de la Unidad 3.

8. ¿Qué característica distintiva tiene el estilo de Schwitters?

_____

_____

9. ¿De qué manera Schwitters usa la palabra *Merz* para describir su obra?

_____

_____

10. ¿En qué se parecen el arte de Schwitters y el de Nevelson?

_____

_____

Unit 3

Answer Key

Vocabulary Practice 1 & 2

Page 47

1. medium
2. palette
3. block
4. plate
5. lithograph

6. collage
7. weaving
8. textiles
9. stitchery

Answer: printmaking

Page 49

1. architect
2. architecture
3. pottery
4. software

5. armature
6. scanner
7. assembling
8. casting

Unit Test, Pages 51 and 52

1. C
2. E
3. D
4. B
5. A
6. Drawings will vary. Students' drawings should show an artist using one of the techniques or media from the unit, with a label that tells what the drawing depicts.
7. Possible answer: Applied art is functional art, such as pottery, jewelry, and textiles. Decorative art includes functional objects that are designed to be ornamental. You might wear functional art and display decorative art in your home.
8. His style is marked by the use of found objects.
9. Schwitters called his creations *Merzbilder*, which means "Merz pictures"—pictures made from castoff items.
10. Possible answer: Both artists use found objects in their artwork.

Práctica de vocabulario 1 y 2

Página 48

1. medio
2. collage
3. bloque
4. placa
5. litografía

6. paleta
7. tejido
8. textiles
9. costura

Respuesta: impresión de grabados

Página 50

Diagonales

1. arquitecto
2. cerámica
3. software

Verticales

6. ensamblar
7. moldear

Horizontales

4. arquitectura
5. escáner

Examen de la unidad, Páginas 53 y 54

1. C
2. E
3. D
4. B
5. A
6. Los dibujos variarán, pero todos deben mostrar a un artista usando una de las técnicas o materiales de esta unidad, con una descripción al pie de la ilustración.
7. Respuesta posible: El arte aplicado es arte funcional, como alfarería, joyería y textiles. El arte decorativo comprende objetos funcionales que son diseñados de modo que sean ornamentales. Uno puede usar arte funcional y puede exhibir en su casa arte decorativo.
8. La característica de su estilo es el uso de objetos encontrados.
9. Schwitters llamó *Merzbilder* a sus creaciones, lo que significa "imágenes de Merz," imágenes creadas con objetos de desecho.
10. Respuesta posible: Ambos artistas usan objetos encontrados en sus obras.

Unit 3

Scoring Rubric

After each studio experience and the portfolio project, complete the following scoring rubric for each student.

Student Name:_____

☐ **Studio 1:** Show Light

☐ **Studio 2:** Combine Tempera with Other Media

☐ **Studio 3:** Print in Combinations

☐ **Studio 4:** Make a Collage with Dimension

☐ **Studio 5:** Make a Mixed-Media Triptych

☐ **Studio 6:** Create Symbols in Bas-Relief

☐ **Studio 7:** Design a Public Landscape

☐ **Studio 8:** Create a Textured Ceramic Jar

☐ **Studio 9:** Colorize a Photograph

☐ **Studio 10:** Design a Web Page

☐ **Portfolio Project:** Make a Multimedia Sculpture

1 Poor	**2 Fair**	**3 Good**	**4 Excellent**
No instructions followed. No effort in problem solving. Shows no understanding of studio or project concept.	Some but not all instructions followed. Some effort in problem solving. Shows some understanding of studio or project concept.	All instructions followed. Basic use of problem-solving skills. Shows understanding of studio or project concept.	All instructions followed. Exceptional use of problem-solving skills. Shows notable creativity and originality in using the studio or project concept.

1 Insuficiente	**2 Aceptable**	**3 Bueno**	**4 Excelente**
No ha seguido las instrucciones. No se ha esforzado en resolver los problemas. No demuestra comprensión del concepto del taller o del proyecto.	Ha seguido algunas instrucciones, pero no todas. Demuestra algún esfuerzo en resolver los problemas. Demuestra alguna comprensión del concepto del taller o del proyecto.	Ha seguido todas las instrucciones. Demuestra un uso básico de destrezas de resolución de problemas. Demuestra comprensión del concepto del taller o del proyecto.	Ha seguido todas las instrucciones. Demuestra un uso excepcional de destrezas de resolución de problemas. Demuestra destacada creatividad y originalidad al aplicar el concepto del taller o del proyecto.

Unit 3

Unit 3 Self-Check

Unit Concepts

1. The art media that I enjoy using most are _____

   because _____

   _____ .

2. I think the most challenging techniques to use are _____

   because _____

   _____ .

Studios and Portfolio Project

3. Which studio/project was the most difficult? Why?

   _____

4. What would you do differently next time?

   _____

5. Which studio/project was the most creative for expressing your ideas?

   _____

6. What unit concepts helped you with the studios/project?

   _____

7. What did you learn from creating the artworks in this unit?

   _____

8. What technique would you like to explore further?

   _____

Unit 3

Unidad 3 Autoevaluación

Conceptos de la unidad

1. El material o medio que más disfruto usar es _____

   porque _____

   _____.

2. Creo que las técnicas más difíciles de usar son _____

   porque _____

   _____.

Talleres y proyecto para el portafolio

3. ¿Qué taller o proyecto fue el más difícil? ¿Por qué?

   _____

4. ¿Qué harías de manera diferente la próxima vez?

   _____

5. ¿Qué taller o proyecto te permitió expresar tus ideas de manera más creativa? ¿Por qué?

   _____

6. ¿Qué conceptos aprendidos en esta unidad te sirvieron de ayuda para realizar los talleres o el proyecto?

   _____

7. ¿Qué aprendiste al crear tus obras de arte de esta unidad?

   _____

8. ¿Qué técnica te gustaría explorar más?

   _____

Curriculum Connection

Science

Materials

- ☐ science textbooks
- ☐ computer with Internet access
- ☐ chart paper, pens, pencils, markers

Understanding Light Have students work in small groups to research the electromagnetic spectrum of light. Students should trace the spectrum from gamma rays to ultraviolet to radio waves, explaining their typical use. Groups can create a chart or other visual display to show their findings. Remember to guide students in using safe Internet practices. ⓢ

Music

Materials

- ☐ p. 110 of Student Edition
- ☐ different types of music
- ☐ CD player, cassette player
- ☐ drawing paper, drawing media

Automatic Drawing Review the information about automatic drawing on page 110. Then play three to five minute selections from different types of music and have students experiment with automatic drawing, using the music as inspiration. After each selection, have volunteers share their creations and explain how the music inspired their drawings.

Health

Materials

- ☐ p. 122 of Student Edition
- ☐ large plastic garbage bags
- ☐ disposable plastic gloves ⓢ

Reinvent and Recycle As a class, reread the Look and Compare on page 122. Then plan a class drive to clean up the school grounds, local park, or other community area. Students can work in teams to collect everyday objects to use in collages as they dispose of trash and recycle glass, paper, and plastic. Remind students to wear gloves and use caution as they pick up trash.

Language Arts

Materials

- ☐ p. 126 of Student Edition
- ☐ writing paper
- ☐ pens or pencils

Street Story Have students write a short story based on Faith Ringgold's *Street Story Quilt #1, 2, and 3*. Students can describe all the action they see or focus on one small part of the quilt. When everyone is finished writing, have volunteers read their stories to the class as students study the quilt.

Culminating Activities

Museum Project: Art Media Treasure Hunt

Take students to an art museum or on a virtual tour to find as many examples of art media as they can. For a virtual tour, see the Web site for The Fine Art Museums of San Francisco (www.thinker.org). Remember to guide students in using safe Internet practices. ⓢ

Before You Go

Remind students of what they learned in Unit 3 about art media and techniques. Explain to the class that they will visit a real or a virtual museum to find as many different techniques as they can, including painting, drawing, printmaking, sculpture, collage, weaving, architecture, photography, and computer design. Have students identify the media used for each technique.

During the Visit

Review the principles of art on the tour.

- Have students locate an artwork that appeals to them.
- Have them write down the title of the artwork, the artist's name, and the technique and media used to create it.
- Challenge students to see how many different techniques they can locate and verify.

When You Return

As students share their lists, compile a class list. Discuss which techniques were used most often and which types of media were the most popular.

Performing Arts: Town Architectural Tour

After students complete Lesson 7 on page 132, have them create a tour of the different forms of architecture in their area.

Prepare

Arrange students in small groups. Have each group select one building in their town and analyze its architecture. Then have each group perform the following tasks:

- Build a model of the building or draw it.
- Research and analyze the building's architectural style.
- Prepare a brief speech to give on the tour to explain the building's style, structure, use, and importance.

Practice

Allow the groups sufficient time to prepare their material and practice their tours.

Perform

Have students arrange the models or drawings in the appropriate places to represent the town. Then have each group give its building tour. If possible, invite a local historian, architect, or elected official to attend.

Overview

Many prominent artists are featured in Unit 4, such as:

Anne Vallayer-Coster

18th century court painter

Anne Vallayer-Coster. *Still Life With Coral, Shells, and Lithophytes,* 1769. Oil on canvas, 51⅛ by 38 inches. Musée du Louvre, Paris.

Unit Contents

Materials List 62
Family Letter 63
Vocabulary Practice 1 65
Vocabulary Practice 2 67
Unit Test 69
Answer Key 73
Scoring Rubric 74
Self-Check 75
Curriculum Connection 77
Culminating Activities 78

Unit Vocabulary

1. creative process, non-objective, features
2. effigy vessels
3. genre scenes
4. still life
6. landscapes, panorama
7. cityscape

Unit 4

Materials List

Below are materials needed for each studio experience and the portfolio project. Materials followed by an * are items families might be able to donate.

Studio 1: Draw an Expressive Portrait

- [ ] full-sized photographs of people's faces*
- [ ] scissors ⚠
- [ ] nontoxic rubber cement
- [ ] drawing paper, drawing pencils
- [ ] colored pencils or pastels

Studio 2: Creative Expressions in Clay

- [ ] newsprint
- [ ] pencils and erasers
- [ ] self-hardening or ceramic clay
- [ ] clay tools and slip

Studio 3: Paint a Group Portrait

- [ ] paper
- [ ] vine charcoal
- [ ] tempera paints (one color plus black and white) and paintbrushes

Studio 4: Paint a Personal Collection Still Life

- [ ] pencils or vine charcoal
- [ ] 12" × 18" white paper, newsprint
- [ ] tempera paints and paintbrushes
- [ ] water containers*
- [ ] various objects to arrange in a still life*

Studio 5: Create an Animal Print

- [ ] newsprint
- [ ] blunt pencils
- [ ] clean plastic foam meat trays*
- [ ] black printing ink and brayers
- [ ] 9" × 12" colored construction paper

Studio 6: Make a Landscape Postcard

- [ ] Sketchbook Journals or sketch paper
- [ ] white cardstock or posterboard
- [ ] pencils and erasers
- [ ] tempera or watercolor paint
- [ ] small paintbrushes, water containers*
- [ ] markers, rulers, scissors ⚠

Studio 7: Draw a Cityscape

- [ ] photographs or videos featuring cities and buildings*
- [ ] 12" × 18" white paper
- [ ] pencils and rulers
- [ ] crayons or pastels, colored markers
- [ ] spray fixative (optional) ⚠

Studio 8: Create Computer Fantasy Art

- [ ] magazines
- [ ] scissors ⚠
- [ ] computer, painting software, scanner, and printer or 12" × 18" white paper
- [ ] paint, paintbrushes, and water containers*
- [ ] colored pencils and markers
- [ ] glue sticks or other adhesives

Portfolio Project: Create Self-Portraits in Three Styles

- [ ] mirrors ⚠
- [ ] newsprint
- [ ] 4 sheets of 12" × 18" heavy white drawing paper per student
- [ ] various drawing and painting media
- [ ] computer, scanner, and painting software

⚠ Educate students about safe use of these materials.

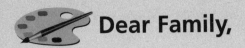 **Dear Family,**

In this unit, students will learn about the creative process from understanding how an idea takes shape to evaluating the final artwork. Students will discover how artists use subject matter and style to express their ideas and extend their knowledge to help them develop their own individual styles.

Students will study fine artworks, including those by Gilbert Stuart, James Whistler, Arnie Fisk, and Anne Vallayer-Coster. A librarian or teacher can help you locate information about these artists.

During this unit, your child will create artworks such as an expressive portrait, expressions in clay, a group portrait, and a landscape postcard. I invite you to display these artworks at home. I am gathering the materials we need to begin. If you would like to donate any of the following items, please send them in by the date of _____:

_____

_____

_____

_____

When your child brings home an artwork, ask questions such as the following:

- Where did you get your idea for this artwork?
- How did you develop this idea? How did sketches, notes, or models help you?
- What was the most interesting part of creating this artwork?

Thank you for experiencing art with your child!

Sincerely,

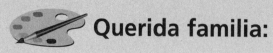 **Querida familia:**

En esta unidad, los estudiantes aprenderán de qué se trata el proceso creativo, desde la comprensión de cómo toma forma una idea hasta la evaluación de la obra finalizada. Los estudiantes descubrirán cómo los artistas usan el tema y el estilo para expresar sus ideas. Además, el ampliar sus conocimientos les facilitará el desarrollo de un estilo propio.

Se estudiarán obras de arte, incluyendo las de Gilbert Stuart, James Whistler, Arnie Fisk y Anne Vallayer-Coster. Un(a) maestro(a) o bibliotecario(a) puede ayudarle a encontrar más información sobre estos artistas.

Durante el transcurso de esta unidad, su niño(a) creará sus propias obras de arte, como un retrato expresivo, expresiones en arcilla, un retrato de grupo y una postal con un paisaje. Invito a la familia a exhibir estas obras en casa. Estoy reuniendo los materiales que necesitamos para comenzar. Si usted deseara donar alguno de los siguientes artículos, por favor envíelos antes de la fecha _____:

_____

_____

_____

_____

Cuando su niño(a) traiga sus trabajos a casa, hágale preguntas como las siguientes:

- ¿En qué te inspiraste para crear esta obra?
- ¿Cómo desarrollaste la idea? ¿De qué manera te sirvieron los bocetos, las notas o los modelos?
- ¿Qué parte de la creación de esta obra fue la más interesante? Explica tu respuesta.

¡Gracias por participar en la experiencia del arte con su niño(a)!

Atentamente,

Name _____

Vocabulary Practice 1

Draw a line from each word or phrase to its definition.

1. creative process   A. paintings from everyday life

2. non-objective   B. characteristics that stand out

3. features   C. the steps every artist goes through to pick a subject and medium

4. effigy vessels   D. portrait pots

5. genre scenes   E. having no recognizable subject

In the box below, draw a genre scene showing how you and your friends like to spend your time.

6.

✔ Turn the paper over. Describe how you use the creative process to make art.

Práctica de vocabulario 1

Une con una línea cada palabra con su definición.

1. proceso creativo

2. no objetivo

3. rasgos

4. vasijas de efigie

5. escenas genéricas

A. pinturas sobre la vida cotidiana

B. características que se destacan

C. los pasos que sigue un artista al escojer un tema y un medio

D. recipientes con retratos

E. que no tiene un tema específico que se pueda identificar

En el recuadro de abajo, dibújate con amigo haciendo una de las actividades que más les gustan.

6.

 En la parte de atrás de la hoja, describe cómo aplicas el proceso creativo para realizar obras de arte.

Vocabulary Practice 2

Use each word or phrase in a sentence that relates to art or artwork as described in this unit.

1. still life _____

_____

2. landscapes _____

_____

3. panorama _____

_____

4. cityscape _____

_____

Draw a landscape. On the lines below your drawing, write a sentence that explains the feeling or mood that your drawing evokes.

5.

_____

_____

☑ On the back of this page, draw a cityscape.

Unit 4

Unit 4

Práctica de vocabulario 2

Usa cada palabra en una oración relacionada con el arte o con una obra de arte que explique su significado.

1. naturaleza muerta _____

_____

2. paisajes _____

_____

3. panorama _____

_____

4. paisaje urbano _____

_____

Dibuja un paisaje. En las líneas de abajo, escribe una oración que explique el estado de ánimo que transmite tu dibujo.

5.

_____

_____

☑ Dibuja un paisaje urbano en la parte de atrás de la hoja.

Name _____

Unit Test

Complete each sentence with a word or phrase from the Word Bank. Use each word only once.

> non-objective   landscapes   features
> genre scenes   panorama

1. Albert Bierstadt, William H. Johnson, and Georgia O'Keeffe painted

   _____ that show the beauty and majesty of the outdoors.

2. Artists use size and proportion to capture their subjects' _____,

   including their noses, mouths, eyes, and ears.

3. The series of _____ showed people having fun in their everyday

   lives, eating, dancing, and talking.

4. The broad _____ showed the wide open prairie, acres of wheat as

   far as the eye could see.

5. We could not find the subject in the _____ painting.

Draw a still life.

6.

Unit Test

Write a short paragraph that compares and contrasts landscapes to cityscapes. Give examples of each one.

7. _____

_____

_____

_____

_____

_____

_____

Think about Realism and Abstraction in Still Lifes, as described in Look and Compare in Unit 4.

Write **T** if the statement is true. Write **F** if the statement is false.

_____ 8. Anne Vallayer-Coster and Rufino Tamayo painted still lifes that were very similar in style.

_____ 9. Vallayer-Coster is known for capturing fine details that make her paintings highly realistic.

_____ 10. Tamayo used bright colors in abstract works that combined European styles with Mexican folk art.

Examen de la unidad

Completa las oraciones con palabras o frases del Banco de palabras. Usa cada término una sola vez.

paisaje urbano	paisajes	rasgos
escenas genéricas	panorámica	

1. Albert Bierstdat, William H. Johnson y Georgia O'Keeffe pintaron

   _____ en los que describen la belleza y majestuosidad

   de la naturaleza.

2. Los artistas aplican el tamaño y la proporción para captar los

   _____ de sus sujetos, por ejemplo, sus narices, bocas, ojos y orejas.

3. El _____ mostraba gente haciendo actividades de la vida diaria

   en la ciudad.

4. En esta amplia vista _____ se ve la extensa pradera, cubierta de

   acres y acres de trigo hasta donde llega la vista.

5. No podíamos descubrir cuál era el tema de aquella pintura de _____.

Dibuja una naturaleza muerta.

6.

Examen de la unidad

Escribe un párrafo corto en el que compares y contrastes paisajes naturales y urbanos. Da ejemplos de cada uno.

7. _____

_____

_____

_____

_____

_____

Piensa en "El realismo y la abstracción en las naturalezas muertas" que se describe en la sección Mira y compara de la Unidad 4.

Escribe **V** si la oración es verdadera y **F** si es falsa.

_____ **8.** Anne Vallayer–Coster y Rufino Tamayo pintaron naturalezas muertas de estilos muy parecidos.

_____ **9.** Vallayer–Coster se destaca por capturar hasta los más pequeños detalles en sus pinturas, lo que las hace muy realistas.

_____ **10.** En sus obras abstractas, que combinaban estilos europeos con el arte folclórico mexicano, Tamayo usó colores vivos.

Answer Key

Vocabulary Practice 1 & 2

Page 65

1. C
2. E
3. B
4. D
5. A

6. Drawing should show students engaged in a typical pastime.

Page 67

1. Possible answer: A still life can be realistic or abstract.
2. Possible answer: Landscapes capture the beauty of the natural environment.
3. Possible answer: The panorama was a wide, open view of the mountain range.
4. Possible answer: The cityscape showed downtown Los Angeles.
5. Drawing should show a natural outdoor scene. Caption should describe mood that is conveyed

Unit Test, Pages 69 and 70

1. landscapes
2. features
3. genre scenes
4. panorama
5. non-objective
6. Drawing should show an arrangement of inanimate objects such as fruit, baskets, and books.
7. Possible answer: A landscape shows a view of natural the scenery, while a cityscape is shows a city scene. Students can cite *The Rocky Mountains, Lander's Peak, 1863* by Albert Bierstadt as an example of a landscape and *Street Scene* by Sidney Goodman for the cityscape.
8. F
9. T
10. T

Práctica de vocabulario 1 y 2

Página 66

1. C
2. E
3. B
4. D
5. A

6. Los dibujos deberán mostrar a los estudiantes realizando alguna de sus actividades favoritas.

Página 68

1. Respuesta posible: Una naturaleza muerta puede ser figurativa o abstracta.
2. Respuesta posible: Los paisajes capturan la belleza del ambiente natural.
3. Respuesta posible: La panorámica era una amplia vista de la cordillera.
4. Respuesta posible: El cuadro era un paisaje urbano del centro de Los Ángeles.
5. Los dibujos deberán mostrar un paisaje natural. El pie de página debe describir el ambiente acordado por los estudiantes.

Examen de la unidad, Páginas 71 y 72

1. paisajes
2. rasgos
3. paisaje urbano
4. panorámica
5. escenas genéricas
6. Los dibujos deberán mostrar un arreglo de objetos inanimados, como frutas, canastos y libros.
7. Respuesta posible: En un paisaje natural se ve una escena de la naturaleza, mientras que en el paisaje urbano se ve una escena de la ciudad. Los estudiantes pueden mencionar *The Rocky Mountains, Lander's Peak, 1863*, de Albert Bierstadt como ejemplo de paisaje natural, y *Street Scene* de Sidney Goodman como ejemplo de paisaje urbano.
8. F
9. V
10. V

Scoring Rubric

After each studio experience and the portfolio project, complete the following scoring rubric for each student.

Student Name: _____

☐ **Studio 1:** Draw an Expressive Portrait

☐ **Studio 2:** Create Expressions in Clay

☐ **Studio 3:** Paint a Group Portrait

☐ **Studio 4:** Paint a Personal Collection Still Life

☐ **Studio 5:** Create an Animal Print

☐ **Studio 6:** Make a Landscape Postcard

☐ **Studio 7:** Draw a Cityscape

☐ **Studio 8:** Create Computer Fantasy Art

☐ **Portfolio Project:** Create Self-Portraits in Three Styles

1 Poor	2 Fair	3 Good	4 Excellent
No instructions followed. No effort in problem solving. Shows no understanding of studio or project concept.	Some but not all instructions followed. Some effort in problem solving. Shows some understanding of studio or project concept.	All instructions followed. Basic use of problem-solving skills. Shows understanding of studio or project concept.	All instructions followed. Exceptional use of problem-solving skills. Shows notable creativity and originality in using the studio or project concept.

1 Insuficiente	2 Aceptable	3 Bueno	4 Excelente
No ha seguido las instrucciones. No se ha esforzado en resolver los problemas. No demuestra comprensión del concepto del taller o del proyecto.	Ha seguido algunas instrucciones, pero no todas. Demuestra algún esfuerzo en resolver los problemas. Demuestra alguna comprensión del concepto del taller o del proyecto.	Ha seguido todas las instrucciones. Demuestra un uso básico de destrezas de resolución de problemas. Demuestra comprensión del concepto del taller o del proyecto.	Ha seguido todas las instrucciones. Demuestra un uso excepcional de destrezas de resolución de problemas. Demuestra destacada creatividad y originalidad al aplicar el concepto del taller o del proyecto.

Name _____

Unit 4 Self-Check

Unit Concepts

1. I learned about _____

_____.

Here are two things I learned: _____.

2. To me, the most interesting part of the creative process is _____

because _____

_____.

Studios and Portfolio Project

3. Which studio/project was the most difficult? Why?

_____

4. What would you do differently next time?

_____

5. Which studio/project was the most creative for expressing your ideas?

_____

6. What unit concepts helped you with the studios/project?

_____

7. What did you learn from creating the artworks in this unit?

_____

8. What technique would you like to explore further?

_____

Unidad 4 Autoevaluación

Conceptos de la unidad

1. He aprendido sobre _____

_____.

   Dos de las cosas que aprendí fueron: _____.

2. Para mí, la parte más interesante del proceso creativo es _____

   porque _____

_____.

Talleres y proyecto para el portafolio

3. ¿Qué taller o proyecto fue el más difícil? ¿Por qué?

_____

4. ¿Qué harías de manera diferente la próxima vez?

_____

5. ¿Qué taller o proyecto te permitió expresar tus ideas de manera más creativa?
   ¿Por qué?

_____

6. ¿Qué conceptos aprendidos en esta unidad te sirvieron de ayuda para realizar los
   talleres o el proyecto?

_____

7. ¿Qué aprendiste al crear tus obras de arte de esta unidad?

_____

8. ¿Qué técnica te gustaría explorar más?

_____

Curriculum Connection

Social Studies

Materials

☐ computer with Internet access
☐ pencils, paper, markers

Portrait Pots Have students work in small groups to research ancient and modern cultures that decorate their pottery with portraits. Guide each group to focus on one specific culture and to include pictures and other visuals in their reports. Groups can post their results on the class Web page or in print reports. Remember to guide students in using safe Internet practices. ⚠

Math

Materials

☐ magazines, newspapers
☐ p. 156 of Student Edition
☐ ruler, scissors ⚠
☐ writing paper, pens or pencils

Proportions in Popular Culture Have students review the information about features in Lesson 1. Then have pairs of students cut out pictures of popular entertainers from newspapers and magazines, measure their features, and analyze the results. Students can then draw conclusions about our ideal of beauty and discuss their observations as a class.

Visual Culture

Materials

☐ pp. 164 and 165 of Student Edition
☐ writing paper, pens or pencils

Parisian Life Have students work independently to analyze *Luncheon of the Boating Party* on page 165 to discover what it reveals about life in Paris in the late 1800s. Encourage students to study the painting closely, focusing on the characters' dress, posture, emotions, and expression as well as the food, cutlery, tent, and colors. Students can use the analysis of *The Eve of St. Nicholas* on page 164 as a model. Students should make an outline or take notes for a class discussion.

Technology

Materials

☐ computer with Internet access
☐ graphic arts software
☐ printer paper, printer

Computer Landscape or Cityscape Have students work in pairs to create a local landscape or cityscape. Encourage them to start with an online map, which can provide accurate measurements and key landmarks. Then students can use the graphic arts software to complete the activity. Remember to guide students in using safe Internet practices. ⚠

Unit 4

Culminating Activities

Museum Project: Tracing the Steps in the Creative Process

Take students to an art museum or on a virtual tour to find how an artist moves from idea to development to evaluation. For a virtual tour, see the Web site for The Seattle Art Museum (**www.seattleartmuseum.org**). Remember to guide students in using safe Internet practices. Ⓢ

Before You Go

Have students suggest ways to use what they learned about the creative process in this unit as they view works of art. Tell students that they will visit a real or a virtual museum to explore stages in the creative process by analyzing sketches, models, and drafts to see how art unfolds.

During the Visit

On the tour, review the steps in the creative process.

- Ask each student to find an exhibit that shows the creative process of one specific work of art. The display should include early studies, artist's notes, models, various drafts, and so on.

- Have students list the title, artist, and number and form of the drafts.
- Have students analyze how the artist developed the artwork from stage to stage. Ask students what the early drafts reveal about the artist's thinking and why certain parts were dropped and others retained.

When You Return

Students can share their analyses with the class and discuss how different artists responded to the creative process.

Performing Arts: Portrait Monologues

After students complete Studio 1 on page 159, have them perform monologues using the portraits.

Prepare

Have each student complete the following tasks:

- Study the expressive portrait made in Studio 1 and decide what it reveals about the character.
- Name the character and write a monologue about the character's life, including key events that reveal personality traits and provoke an emotional response.
- Edit the monologue to last between two and three minutes.

Practice

Have students practice their monologues. Remind them to address the audience and speak loudly, slowly, and clearly.

Perform

Have students perform their monologues as they display their portraits. If possible, set up the portraits in a gallery and record the monologues so that viewers can listen to them.

Overview

Many prominent artists are featured in Unit 5, such as:

*Unknown ancient
Mayan artist*

Artist unknown. *Ruler Dressed As Chac-Xib-Chac and the Holmul Dancer,* ca. A.D. 600–800. Ceramic with traces of paint, height 9⅜ inches. The Kimbell Art Museum, Fort Worth, TX.

Unit Contents

Materials List. 80

Family Letter 81

Vocabulary Practice 1 83

Vocabulary Practice 2 85

Unit Test. 87

Answer Key 91

Scoring Rubric. 92

Self-Check 93

Curriculum Connection 95

Culminating Activities 96

Unit Vocabulary

1. art historians, pre-Columbian art
2. hieroglyphics
3. Classical style, pediment, frieze
5. Middle Ages, cathedrals, Gothic, interlace
7. obsidian
8. calligraphy
9. terra cotta, bronze, plaques, lost wax casting
10. Op Art, Pop Art

Materials List

Below are materials needed for each studio experience and the portfolio project. Materials followed by an * are items families might be able to donate.

Studio 1: Paint an Animal Scene on Stone

- ☐ newsprint and pencils
- ☐ flat, rough stones, at least 7" wide, or terra-cotta or limestone quarry tiles*
- ☐ black or brown acrylic paint
- ☐ round paintbrushes, water containers*
- ☐ umber, sienna, and ocher chalk pastels
- ☐ hog bristle or other stiff paintbrushes

Studio 2: Paint an Egyptian Scene

- ☐ rice paper, papyrus, or watercolor paper
- ☐ pencils
- ☐ paint, paintbrushes, water containers*

Studio 3: Create an Architectural Frieze

- ☐ newsprint
- ☐ pencils or vine charcoal
- ☐ 4 sheets of 12" × 18" heavy white paper per student
- ☐ watercolors, paintbrushes, water containers*

Studio 4: Sculpt a Roman-Style Portrait

- ☐ photographs of students' subjects
- ☐ 5" × 17" blocks of clay, plus extra
- ☐ clay tools, water containers*
- ☐ acrylic paint, tempera paint, or glaze and paintbrushes

Studio 5: Create an Interlace Design

- ☐ newsprint
- ☐ white construction paper
- ☐ pencils, erasers, and fine-tipped markers
- ☐ watercolors, paintbrushes, water containers*
- ☐ rulers

Studio 6: Design a Door-front Relief

- ☐ 1 large sheet of heavy white drawing paper per student
- ☐ brown and black ink or watercolors
- ☐ paintbrushes, water containers*
- ☐ small containers for ink washes* (optional)

Studio 7: Create a Pre-Columbian Animal Vessel

- ☐ newsprint and pencils
- ☐ papier-mâché paste or liquid starch*
- ☐ masking tape, newspaper*
- ☐ plastic wrap or balloons* (optional)
- ☐ tempera or acrylic paint, paintbrushes

Studio 8: Paint a Chinese Landscape

- ☐ white craft paper, wooden dowels*
- ☐ pencils, glue
- ☐ watercolors and ink
- ☐ paintbrushes and water containers*

Studio 9: Create a Personal Plaque

- ☐ 12" × 14" sheets of cardboard and cardboard pieces*
- ☐ glue, utility knives, scissors ⚠
- ☐ miscellaneous found objects*
- ☐ tempera or acrylic paint
- ☐ metallic paint paste and cotton cloths*

Studio 10: Create an Op Art Drawing

- ☐ white paper
- ☐ fine-tipped black pens
- ☐ glue sticks, scissors ⚠
- ☐ black construction paper
- ☐ ruler, drawing tools* (optional)

Portfolio Project: Create a Pop Art Meal

- ☐ pencils and markers
- ☐ construction paper, newsprint
- ☐ glue, scissors ⚠
- ☐ papier-mâché paste
- ☐ newspaper strips
- ☐ self-hardening clay
- ☐ acrylic paint

⚠ Educate students about safe use of these materials.

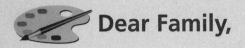 **Dear Family,**

In this unit, students will learn about art through the ages from cultures around the world, including the Americas, Europe and the Mediterranean countries, parts of the Middle East, and Asia. Students will also explore the struggles that many artists have endured to express their ideas. This overview of art history will help students bring a wider perspective to their own artistic creations.

Fine artworks, including those by Michelangelo Buonarroti, Leonardo da Vinci, Lorenzo Ghiberti, Richard Anuskiewicz, and Lucas Samaras, will be studied. A librarian or teacher can help you locate additional information about these artists.

During this unit, your child will create artworks such as an interlace design, a door-front relief, a Chinese landscape, and a personal plaque. I invite you to display these artworks at home. I am gathering the materials we need to begin. If you would like to donate any of the following items, please send them in by the date of _____:

_____

_____

_____

_____

When your child brings home an artwork, ask questions such as the following:
- What tradition does your artwork belong to? Explain the elements that you drew from the history of art that you studied.
- How does this artwork reflect our culture?
- What was the most challenging part of creating this artwork? Why?

Thank you for experiencing art with your child!

Sincerely,

 # Querida familia:

En esta unidad, los estudiantes aprenderán acerca de la historia del arte, a través del tiempo y en distintas culturas de todo el mundo. También explorarán las dificultades que muchos artistas han tenido que enfrentar para expresar sus ideas. Este vistazo general a la historia del arte dará a los estudiantes una perspectiva más amplia, la que podrán aplicar a sus propias creaciones artísticas.

Se estudiarán obras de arte, incluyendo algunas de Michelangelo Buonarroti, Leonardo da Vinci, Lorenzo Ghiberti, Richard Anuskiewicz y Lucas Samaras. Un bibliotecario(a) o maestro(a) puede ayudarle a encontrar más información sobre estos artistas.

Durante el transcurso de esta unidad, su niño(a) también creará obras de arte, como una letra capitular, el relieve para una puerta, un paisaje chino y una placa personal. Estoy reuniendo los materiales que necesitamos para comenzar. Si usted deseara donar alguno de los siguientes artículos, por favor envíelos antes de la fecha _____:

_____

_____

_____

_____

Cuando su niño(a) traiga sus trabajos a casa, hágale preguntas como las siguientes:

- ¿A qué tradición pertenece tu obra? Explica qué elementos de la historia del arte has incorporado a ella.
- ¿De qué manera refleja esta obra nuestra cultura?
- ¿Qué fue lo más difícil al crear esta obra? ¿Por qué?

Gracias por participar en la experiencia del arte con su niño(a)!

Atentamente,

Vocabulary Practice 1

Complete each sentence with a word or phrase from the Word Bank. Use each word only once.

> art historians   hieroglyphics   pediment
> Middle Ages   cathedrals

1. The art of the _____ shows a great emphasis on religion, as reflected in the many beautiful churches built during that era.

2. Large, elaborate churches, also called _____ , have delicate stone spires and other fancy stone work.

3. It took many years for modern scholars to figure out _____ , the ancient Egyptian system of picture writing.

4. The stone _____ that supports the roof is adorned with Classical sculptures of heroic figures.

5. Studying the culture and history of a region helps _____ understand how people express themselves creatively.

☑ Turn the paper over. Write a sentence about art history using an interlace design to create the initial letter.

Práctica de vocabulario 1

Completa las oraciones con una palabra o frase del recuadro. Usa cada término una sola vez.

> historiadores del arte   jeroglíficos   frontón
> Edad Media   catedrales

1. El arte de la _____ hace mucho énfasis en temas religiosos, como se ve en las numerosas y hermosas iglesias construidas en esa época.

2. Las iglesias grandes, llamadas _____ , tienen complejas columnas de piedra y otros elaborados trabajos de albañilería.

3. Para descifrar los _____ egipcios, los científicos contemporáneos pasaron muchos años estudiando ese antiguo sistema de escritura.

4. El _____ de piedra que sostiene el techo está adornado con esculturas clásicas de héroes.

5. Los _____ entienden cómo los pueblos se expresan creativamente al estudiar la cultura y la historia de una región.

✔ En la parte de atrás de la hoja, escribe una oración sobre la historia del arte. Haz la primera litra en estilo capitular.

Vocabulary Practice 2

Use each word or phrase in a sentence that relates to the art techniques or artworks described in this unit.

1. calligraphy _____

_____

2. lost wax casting _____

_____

3. obsidian _____

_____

4. terra cotta_____

_____

5. bronze_____

_____

Draw an example of Op Art. On the lines below your drawing, write a sentence that explains why your drawing can be considered Op Art.

6.

_____

_____

☑ On the back of this paper, draw a plaque for your school or community. Explain the symbols you used.

Unit 5

Unit 5

Práctica de vocabulario 2

Emplea cada palabra en una oración relacionada con las técnicas u obras de arte que se describen en esta unidad.

1. caligrafía _____

_____

2. moldear la cera _____

_____

3. obsidiana _____

_____

4. terracota _____

_____

5. bronce _____

_____

Dibuja un ejemplo de Op Art. En las líneas de abajo, escribe una oración en la que expliques por qué tu dibujo puede considerarse Op Art.

6.

_____

_____

☑ En la parte de atrás de la hoja, diseña una placa para tu escuela o comunidad. Explica los símbolos que usaste.

Unit Test

Write **T** if the sentence is true or **F** if the sentence is false.

_____ 1. Pre-Columbian art developed in ancient Greece and Rome.

_____ 2. A frieze, or a band of sculpture, runs along the top of a building.

_____ 3. The Middle Ages lasted from about A.D. 400 to about A.D. 1300.

_____ 4. The ancient Egyptians used a form of picture writing called plaques.

_____ 5. Gothic architecture often has many decorative details such as carvings, angels, and tall spires.

Draw a Classical style building. Label the pediment.

6.

Unit 5

Unit Test

Write a short paragraph that compares and contrasts hieroglyphics and calligraphy.
Give examples of when and where each one was used.

7. _____

_____

_____

_____

_____

_____

_____

_____

_____

Think about the two temples described in Look and Compare in Unit 5. Complete each
sentence with a word or phrase.

8. Chichén Itzá was founded around A.D. 500 by the _____
   in the Yucatán.

9. The rulers of the ancient Khmer empire in Cambodia built huge structures
   for the purpose of _____.

10. Both temples are made of _____ and covered with
    beautiful relief sculptures.

Examen de la unidad

Junto a cada oración, escribe **V** si es verdadero y **F** si es falso.

_____ 1. El arte precolombino se desarrolló en la antigua Grecia y en Roma.

_____ 2. Un friso, que es una franja decorativa esculpida, rodea toda la parte superior del edificio.

_____ 3. La Edad Media se extendió aproximadamente desde el año 400 d.C. hasta el 1300 d.C.

_____ 4. En el antiguo Egipto se usó una forma de escritura con pictogramas llamada placa.

_____ 5. La arquitectura gótica tiene a menudo muchos detalles decorativos como tallados, ángeles y altas columnas.

Dibuja una construcción de estilo clásico. Rotula el frontón.

6.

Examen de la unidad

Escribe un párrafo corto en el que compares y contrastes los jeroglíficos y la caligrafía. Menciona ejemplos de cuándo y dónde se usaron unos y otros.

7. _____

_____

_____

_____

_____

_____

_____

_____

_____

_____

Piensa en los dos templos que se describen en la sección Mira y compara de la Unidad 5. Completa las oraciones con palabras o frases.

8. Chichén Itzá fue fundada alrededor del año 500 d.C., por los

_____ del Yucatán.

9. Los gobernantes del antiguo imperio Khmer de Camboya construyeron enormes estructuras con el propósito de _____.

10. Ambos templos están hechos de _____ y cubiertos con bellísimos relieves esculpidos.

Answer Key

Vocabulary Practice 1 & 2

Page 83

1. Middle Ages
2. cathedrals
3. hieroglyphics
4. pediment
5. art historians

Page 85

1. Possible answer: Calligraphy is the ancient art of Chinese writing using ink and a brush.
2. Possible answer: Lost wax casting is used to cast sculptures in brass and bronze.
3. Possible answer: Obsidian is volcanic glass that can be carved.
4. Possible answer: The sculptor liked to work in terra cotta because of the clay's warm reddish-brown color.
5. Possible answer: She cast her metal sculpture in bronze to preserve it through the ages.
6. Drawings will vary but should show an optical illusion.

Unit Test, Pages 87 and 88

1. F
2. T
3. T
4. F
5. T
6. Drawings will vary but should show columns and balance, and the pediment supporting the roof should be labeled.
7. Possible answer: Hieroglyphics and calligraphy are similar because both are systems of writing, both are artistic, and both use symbols. They are different because hieroglyphics were created by the ancient Egyptians and are no longer used today. Calligraphy was created by the Chinese and is still used today.
8. Maya
9. glorifying themselves
10. stone (or rock)

Práctica de vocabulario 1 y 2

Página 84

1. Edad Media
2. catedrales
3. jeroglíficos
4. frontón
5. historiadores del arte

Página 86

1. Respuesta posible: La caligrafía es el antiguo arte chino de escribir con pincel y tinta.
2. Respuesta posible: El moldeado de la cera se usa para fundir esculturas de latón y de bronce.
3. Respuesta posible: La obsidiana es una piedra volcánica cristalina que puede tallarse.
4. Respuesta posible: Al escultor le gustaba trabajar en terracota debido al cálido color marrón rojizo de la arcilla.
5. Respuesta posible: Ella fundió su escultura en bronce para que se conservara a pesar del paso del tiempo.
6. Los dibujos variarán pero deberán mostrar una ilusión óptica.

Examen de la unidad, Páginas 89 y 90

1. F
2. V
3. V
4. F
5. V
6. Los dibujos variarán, pero en ellos deben verse formas equilibradas, columnas y el frontón, que debe estar rotulado con su nombre.
7. Respuesta posible: Los jeroglíficos y la caligrafía tienen en común que ambos son sistemas de escritura, ambos son artísticos y ambos utilizan símbolos. Se diferencian en que los jeroglíficos fueron creados por los antiguos egipcios y ahora están en desuso, y la caligrafía, que fue creada por los chinos, aún se usa.
8. mayas
9. glorificarse a sí mismos
10. piedra

Scoring Rubric

After each studio experience and the portfolio project, complete the following scoring rubric for each student.

Student Name:_____

☐ **Studio 1:** Paint an Animal Scene on Stone
☐ **Studio 2:** Paint an Egyptian Scene
☐ **Studio 3:** Create an Architectural Frieze
☐ **Studio 4:** Sculpt a Roman-Style Portrait
☐ **Studio 5:** Create an Interlace Design
☐ **Studio 6:** Design a Door-front Relief

☐ **Studio 7:** Create a Pre-Columbian Animal Vessel
☐ **Studio 8:** Paint a Chinese Landscape
☐ **Studio 9:** Create a Personal Plaque
☐ **Studio 10:** Create an Op Art Drawing
☐ **Portfolio Project:** Create a Pop Art Meal

1 Poor	**2 Fair**	**3 Good**	**4 Excellent**
No instructions followed. No effort in problem solving. Shows no understanding of studio or project concept.	Some but not all instructions followed. Some effort in problem solving. Shows some understanding of studio or project concept.	All instructions followed. Basic use of problem-solving skills. Shows understanding of studio or project concept.	All instructions followed. Exceptional use of problem-solving skills. Shows notable creativity and originality in using the studio or project concept.

1 Insuficiente	**2 Aceptable**	**3 Bueno**	**4 Excelente**
No ha seguido las instrucciones. No se ha esforzado en resolver los problemas. No demuestra comprensión del concepto del taller o del proyecto.	Ha seguido algunas instrucciones, pero no todas. Demuestra algún esfuerzo en resolver los problemas. Demuestra alguna comprensión del concepto del taller o del proyecto.	Ha seguido todas las instrucciones. Demuestra un uso básico de destrezas de resolución de problemas. Demuestra comprensión del concepto del taller o del proyecto.	Ha seguido todas las instrucciones. Demuestra un uso excepcional de destrezas de resolución de problemas. Demuestra destacada creatividad y originalidad al aplicar el concepto del taller o del proyecto.

Name _____

Unit 5 Self-Check

Unit Concepts

1. The art through the ages that I found the most interesting was _____

   _____ because _____

   _____.

2. I think the most influential ancient art was _____

   because _____

   _____.

Studios and Portfolio Project

3. Which studio/project was the most difficult? Why?

   _____

4. What would you do differently next time?

   _____

5. Which studio/project was the most creative for expressing your ideas?

   _____

6. What unit concepts helped you with the studios/project?

   _____

7. What did you learn from creating the artworks in this unit?

   _____

8. What technique would you like to explore further?

   _____

Unit 5

Unidad 5 Autoevaluación

Conceptos de la unidad

1. De la historia del arte, lo que me pareció más interesante es _____

_____ porque _____

_____.

2. Creo que el arte de la antigüedad que tuvo más influencia fue el _____

_____

_____ porque _____

_____.

Talleres y proyecto para el portafolio

3. ¿Qué taller o proyecto fue el más difícil? ¿Por qué?

_____

4. ¿Qué harías de manera diferente la próxima vez?

_____

5. ¿Qué taller o proyecto te permitió expresar tus ideas de manera más creativa?

_____

6. ¿Qué conceptos aprendidos en esta unidad te sirvieron de ayuda para realizar los talleres o el proyecto?

_____

7. ¿Qué aprendiste al crear tus obras de arte de esta unidad?

_____

8. ¿Qué técnica te gustaría explorar más?

_____

Curriculum Connection

Research

Materials

☐ computer with Internet access
☐ pencils, paper, markers

Monumental Artworks Have students work in small groups to research explanations for the creation of Stonehenge, the statues on Easter Island, the Colosseum, or other famous monuments from the distant past. Each group should research and evaluate a different artwork. Groups can create slide shows to share their findings with the class. Remember to guide students in using safe Internet practices. ⚠

Math

Materials

☐ computer with Internet access
☐ pencils and graph paper
☐ rulers

How Big are the Pyramids? Have pairs of students compare the size of the Great Pyramid at Giza to other famous architectural masterpieces, such as the Eiffel Tower, the Empire State Building, and Taipei 101. Students can create a bar graph to show the scale of the buildings they choose. Students can research buildings at **www.infoplease.com** and at **www.skyscrapers.com.** Remember to guide students in using safe Internet practices. ⚠

Social Studies

Materials

☐ roll of butcher or craft paper
☐ rulers
☐ pens, pencils, colored markers

The March of History As a class, compile all the historical information in this unit into one time line. Divide the class into ten groups and assign one of the ten lessons to each group. Then come together as a class to plan out the time line and enter each artwork, artist, and event in Unit 5 in its appropriate place on the time line, including small drawings of key works of art. Display the finished time line in the classroom.

Language Arts

Materials

☐ writing paper
☐ pens or pencils

Write a Legend As students learned in Studio 7, the Aztecs often used animals as subjects for sculpture and pottery. The Aztec calendar featured animals, including a lizard, alligator, vulture, eagle, monkey, dog, deer, and rabbit. Have students choose an animal and write a brief legend that explains some aspect of the natural world, such as rain, sunrise, sunset, or earthquakes. Invite volunteers to read their legends to the class.

Culminating Activities

Museum Project: Be an Art Historian

Take students to an art museum or on a virtual tour to delve further into the art of one people, culture, or historical era studied in Unit 5. For a virtual tour, see the Web site for the Saint Louis Art Museum (**www.slam.org**). Remember to guide students in using safe Internet practices. ⚠

Before You Go

Discuss with students how they can build on what they discovered about art through the ages in this unit as they explore one artist, historical era, or culture in greater detail. Tell students that they will visit a real or a virtual museum to enrich their knowledge. They will study art to become an "expert" in an area that interests them.

During the Visit

On the tour, review the cultures and artistic eras studied in Unit 5.

- Ask each student to find an exhibit that focuses on one specific culture or era. The display should include art by different people, artifacts from the era, models of famous structures, and other background information.
- Have students take notes on the new information they learn.
- Have students link these new facts with the information in Unit 5.

When You Return

Have each student give a brief speech describing the new information collected and how it relates to what the class learned in Unit 5.

Performing Arts: Comedy Skits

After students complete the Portfolio Project on page 244, have them work in groups to offer commentary on modern American life.

Prepare

Form small groups. Have each group follow these steps:

- Study the Pop Art meals they made in the Portfolio Project and decide what message or statement they represent about life in America today.
- Arrange the Pop Art meals to convey that message more clearly.
- Write a television-type comedy skit to express that message using the Pop Art meals as the central focus.

Practice

Have students practice their skits. Remind them to speak loudly and clearly, using appropriate body language to underscore their message.

Perform

Have students perform their skits as they display their Pop Art meals. If possible, videotape the skits so that performers can watch themselves later.

Overview

Many prominent artists are featured in Unit 6, such as:

Harold Cohen

Computer artist

Harold Cohen. *Meeting on Gauguin's Beach,* 1988. Computer-drawn image hand-painted with oil on canvas, 90 by 68 inches. Collection of Gordon and Gwen Bell.

Unit Contents

Materials List 98
Family Letter 99
Vocabulary Practice 1 101
Vocabulary Practice 2 103
Unit Test 105
Answer Key 109
Scoring Rubric 110
Self-Check 111
Curriculum Connection 113
Culminating Activities 114

Unit Vocabulary

1. portfolio, applied arts, fine arts, computer artist, hardware, software, pixels, computer-aided design (CAD) software, morphing

2. animator, animation, frame, cel, stop action, storyboard

3. special effects artists, blue screen, matte painting, compositing

4. urban designers, Bauhaus, Postmodern

5. costume designers

6. product designers, function

7. furniture designers, decorative design, Art Nouveau

8. installations

Materials List

Below are materials needed for each studio experience and the portfolio project. Materials followed by an * are items families might be able to donate.

Studio 1: Create a Computer-Generated Self-Portrait

- ☐ digital camera or film camera and scanner
- ☐ computer and image manipulation software
- ☐ glue sticks or two-sided tape
- ☐ posterboard, colored markers

Studio 2: Create a Storyboard

- ☐ paper, white drawing paper
- ☐ pencils and water-based markers

Studio 3: Create a Model

- ☐ newsprint, pencils
- ☐ balsa wood, glue, wire
- ☐ utility knives ⑤
- ☐ found objects*

Studio 4: Design a Postmodern Facade

- ☐ pencils, rulers, protractors
- ☐ 18" × 22" white paper
- ☐ ink and colored pencils
- ☐ watercolors, paintbrushes, and water containers*
- ☐ black posterboard or heavy paper

Studio 5: Design a Costume

- ☐ paper and pencils
- ☐ watercolors, paintbrushes, water containers*
- ☐ water-based markers
- ☐ pens and India ink

Studio 6: Design an Everyday Product

- ☐ newsprint and paper
- ☐ various media*
- ☐ tape and glue
- ☐ ink, dye, or acrylic paint
- ☐ paintbrushes, paper towels, water containers*

Studio 7: Design a Chair with a Natural Form

- ☐ newsprint, pencils, colored markers
- ☐ glue, tape, scissors ⑤
- ☐ sheets of corrugated cardboard and cardboard tubes*
- ☐ various media*
- ☐ acrylic or tempera paint
- ☐ paintbrushes and water containers*

Studio 8: Design an Installation

- ☐ corrugated cardboard sheets*
- ☐ glue, scissors or utility knives ⑤
- ☐ various found objects*
- ☐ acrylic paint, paintbrushes, water containers*

Portfolio Project: Create an Art Careers Exhibit

- ☐ Unit 6 artwork from portfolios
- ☐ 8½" × 11" white paper, pens
- ☐ colored construction paper
- ☐ cardboard or cardboard boxes* (optional)
- ☐ tempera paint and paintbrushes (optional)
- ☐ scissors ⑤
- ☐ tape, glue, glue sticks
- ☐ exhibit location layout sketch

⑤ Educate students about safe use of these materials.

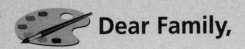 **Dear Family,**

In this unit, students will learn about careers in fine arts and the applied arts, including computer artist, architect, costume designer, furniture designer, and installation artist. Students will learn how to assemble a portfolio to show prospective employers or buyers. In addition, students will have an opportunity to apply some of the skills that professional artists use every day.

Students will study fine artworks, including those by Mies van der Rohe, Rebecca Binder, Calvin Southwell, and Laurene Leon Boym. A librarian or teacher can help you locate additional information about these artists.

During this unit, your child will create artworks such as a computer-generated self-portrait, a model of a vehicle, a design for a costume, and a chair with a natural form. I invite you to display these artworks at home. I am gathering the materials we need to begin. If you would like to donate any of the following items, please send them in by the date of _____:

_____

_____

_____

_____

When your child brings home an artwork, ask questions such as the following:

- Is this an example of an applied art or a fine art?
- In what art career do you think this artwork might be created?
- What was the most interesting part of creating this artwork?

Thank you for experiencing art with your child!

Sincerely,

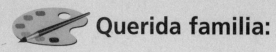 **Querida familia:**

En esta unidad, los estudiantes aprenderán sobre profesiones en las artes decorativas y aplicadas, incluyendo las de diseño de arte por computadora, arquitectura, diseño de vestuario, diseño de muebles y creación de instalaciones de arte. Además, tendrán la oportunidad de aplicar algunas de las destrezas que los artistas profesionales utilizan a diario.

Se estudiarán obras de arte, incluyendo algunas de Mies van der Rohe, Rebecca Binder, Calvin Southwell y Laurene Leon Boym. Puede encontrar más información sobre estos artistas con ayuda de un(a) maestro(a) bibliotecario(a).

Durante el transcurso de esta unidad, su niño(a) también creará obras de arte, como un autorretrato generado por computadora, el modelo de un vehículo, el diseño de un disfraz y una silla con formas naturales. Estoy reuniendo los materiales que necesitamos para comenzar. Si usted deseara donar alguno de los siguientes artículos, por favor envíelos antes de la fecha _____:

_____

_____

_____

_____

Cuando su niño(a) traiga sus trabajos a casa, hágale preguntas como las siguientes:

- ¿Es esta obra un ejemplo de arte decorativo o aplicado?
- ¿Qué profesional del arte crees que podría crear esta obra?
- ¿Cuál fue la parte más interesante de la creación de esta obra?

¡Gracias por participar en la experiencia del arte con su niño(a)!

Atentamente,

Name _____

Vocabulary Practice 1

Complete the crossword puzzle with vocabulary words from Lessons 1 to 3.

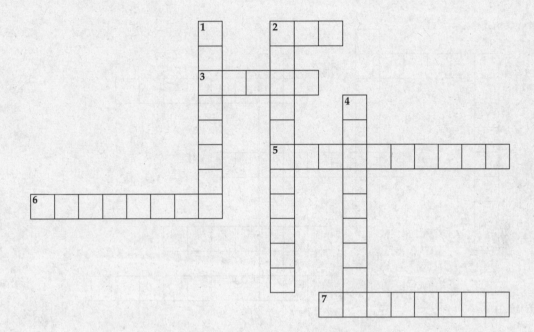

Across

2. picture hand-drawn on transparent acetate

3. one of a series of slightly different images

5. drawing that shows the sequence of scenes in an animation

6. the computer's box and everything in it

7. a technique for gradually changing one image into another

Down

1. the programs that make computer equipment run

2. combining two images

4. a collection of artwork

☑ On the back of this paper, make a new crossword puzzle. Use these vocabulary words: *applied arts, fine arts, pixels, animator, animation, blue screen.*

Unit 6

Práctica de vocabulario 1

Resuelve el crucigrama con palabras del vocabulario de las Lecciones 1 a 3.

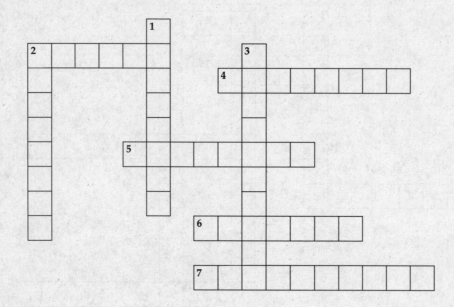

Horizontales

2. cada una de las imágenes de una serie de imágenes apenas diferente una de otra

4. técnica para transformar gradualmente una imagen en otra

5. cuerpo de la computadora y todo lo que contiene

6. pintura hecha a mano sobre acetato transparente

7. dibujo que muestra la secuencia de escenas en una animación

Verticales

1. los programas que hacen funcionar a las computadoras

2. combinar dos imágenes

3. colección que un artista mantiene de sus propias obras de arte

En la parte de atrás de esta hoja, haz un nuevo crucigrama. Usa estas palabras del vocabulario: *artes aplicadas, artes decorativas, pixels, animador, animación, pantalla azul.*

Name _____

Vocabulary Practice 2

Complete each sentence with a word or phrase from the Word Bank. Then use the letters in the boxes to answer the question at the bottom.

> function   Art Nouveau   installations
> Bauhaus   Postmodern

1. ☐ __ __ __ __ __ __ is the German design school that focuses on the purpose of the object.

2. __ __ __ __ __ __ __ __ __ ☐ architects combined elements of many styles in their buildings instead of just contemporary styles.

3. A product's use is often called its __ ☐ __ __ __ __ __ __ .

4. Flowers, leaves, and twisting vines are often used in

    __ ☐ __   __ __ __ __ __ __ __ designs.

5. The __ __ __ __ ☐ __ __ __ __ __ __ __ __ designed especially for the museum had a variety of parts to communicate their message.

Question: What type of architects are interested in the design of an entire city, including roads and parks as well as buildings?

Answer: __ __ __ __ __ designers
    3   4   1   5   2

☑ Turn the paper over. Draw a design for a Postmodern chair. Write a caption to explain what influenced your design.

Práctica de vocabulario 2

Completa cada oración con una de las palabras del recuadro. Luego, usa las letras que queden dentro de los cuadrados para responder a la pregunta de abajo.

> función   Art Nouveau   instalación
> Bauhaus   postmodernos

1. El uso que se da a un objeto es también llamado __ □ __ __ __ __ __ del objeto.

2. En el __ □ __ __ __ __ __ __ __ __ a menudo se utilizan flores, hojas y enredaderas como motivos de decoración.

3. □ __ __ __ __ __ __ es la escuela alemana de diseño que se centra en la finalidad del objeto.

4. Los arquitectos __ __ __ __ __ __ __ __ □ __ __ combinan en sus construcciones elementos de muchos estilos en lugar de usar sólo estilos contemporáneos.

5. La __ __ __ □ __ __ __ __ __ __ __ diseñada especialmente para el museo tenía varias partes que contribuían a transmitir su mensaje.

Pregunta: ¿Qué tipo de arquitectos se interesan en el diseño de una ciudad completa, incluyendo calles, parques y construcciones?

Respuesta: arquitectos __ __ __ a __ i s __ a s
                          1   2   3   4   5

✓ En la parte de atrás de la hoja, dibuja el diseño de una silla postmoderna. Escribe una nota en la que expliques qué influencias ha recibido tu diseño.

Name _____

Unit Test

Draw a line from each word or phrase to its definition.

1. pixels

A. capturing motion through a series of still photographs

2. computer-aided design (CAD) software

B. the dots that form an onscreen image

3. animator

C. the design of furniture and other objects

4. stop action

D. an artist who brings a character to life by drawing the figure in motion

5. decorative design

E. software that allows users to create precise two- and three-dimensional images

In the space below, draw a storyboard for a folktale or fable.

6.

Unit Test

Write a short paragraph that compares and contrasts the applied arts and fine arts. Give examples of each one.

7. _____

_____

_____

_____

_____

_____

Think about computer art as described in Look and Compare in Unit 6. Use phrases or sentences to answer the questions.

8. Why do some artists prefer making computer art to traditional art?

_____

_____

_____

9. What is one way that Harold Cohen's artwork *Untitled* and Sonia Landy Sheridan's *Drawing in Time* are alike?

_____

_____

_____

10. Why is computer art so controversial?

_____

_____

_____

Examen de la unidad

Une con una línea cada palabra o frase con su definición.

1. pixels

A. movimiento capturado mediante una serie de fotografías estáticas

2. programas CAD, de diseño asistido por computadora

B. puntos que forman la imagen en una computadora

3. animador

C. diseño de mobiliario y otros objetos

4. foto fija

D. artista que da vida a un personaje dibujando la figura en movimiento

5. diseño de decoración

E. software o conjunto de programas que permite a los usuarios el crear imágenes en dos y tres dimensiones

En el espacio en blanco, dibuja el *storyboard* para un cuento popular o una fábula.

6.

Unit 6

Examen de la unidad

Escribe un párrafo breve en el que expliques la diferencia entre las artes aplicadas y decorativas. Da ejemplos de cada una.

7. _____

_____

_____

_____

_____

_____

Piensa en el arte por computadora, tal como se describe en la sección Mira y compara de la Unidad 6. Usa frases u oraciones para responder a las preguntas.

8. ¿Por qué algunos artistas prefieren el arte por computadora al arte tradicional?

_____

_____

_____

9. ¿Qué semejanza tienen las obras *Sin título* de Harold Cohen y *Drawing in Time* de Sonia Landy Sheridan?

_____

_____

_____

10. ¿Por qué hay tanta controversia acerca del arte por computadora?

_____

_____

_____

Answer Key

Vocabulary Practice 1 & 2

Page 101

Across	Down
2. cel	1. software
3. frame	2. compositing
5. storyboard	4. portfolio
6. hardware	
7. morphing	

Page 103

1. Bauhaus
2. Postmodern
3. function
4. Art Nouveau
5. installations

Answer: urban

Práctica de vocabulario 1 y 2

Página 102

Horizontales	Verticales
2. cuadro	1. software
4. morphing	2. componer
5. hardware	3. portafolio
6. celofán	
7. storyboard	

Página 104

1. función
2. Art Nouveau
3. Bauhaus
4. posmodernos
5. instalación

Respuesta: urbanistas

Unit Test, Pages 105 and 106

1. B
2. E
3. D
4. A
5. C
6. Drawings should show the sequence of events in the story.
7. Possible answer: Applied arts are the functional branch of arts, such as architecture and costume design. Fine arts include drawing, painting, and sculpting and are designed to express the artist's vision.
8. Possible answer: They are attracted by the flexibility of the medium.
9. Possible answer: Both are made by artists using computers.
10. Possible answer: Some people question whether computer art is art at all because the creative process is mechanically manipulated.

Examen de la unidad, Páginas 107 y 108

1. B
2. E
3. D
4. A
5. C
6. Los dibujos deben mostrar los sucesos del cuento en orden.
7. Respuesta posible: Las artes aplicadas son las artes funcionales, como arquitectura y diseño de vestuario. Entre las artes visuales están la escultura, el dibujo y la pintura, diseñados para expresar la visión del artista.
8. Respuesta posible: Les atrae la flexibilidad del medio.
9. Respuesta posible: Ambas obras fueron creadas por medio de computadoras.
10. Respuesta posible: Algunos se preguntan si el arte computarizado es arte o no, ya que el proceso creativo es manipulado mecánicamente.

Scoring Rubric

After each studio experience and the portfolio project, complete the following scoring rubric for each student.

Student Name:_____

- [ ] **Studio 1:** Create a Computer-Generated Self-Portrait
- [ ] **Studio 2:** Create a Storyboard
- [ ] **Studio 3:** Create a Model
- [ ] **Studio 4:** Design a Postmodern Facade
- [ ] **Studio 5:** Design a Costume

- [ ] **Studio 6:** Design an Everyday Product
- [ ] **Studio 7:** Design a Chair with a Natural Form
- [ ] **Studio 8:** Design an Installation
- [ ] **Portfolio Project:** Create an Art Careers Exhibit

1 Poor	**2 Fair**	**3 Good**	**4 Excellent**
No instructions followed. No effort in problem solving. Shows no understanding of studio or project concept.	Some but not all instructions followed. Some effort in problem solving. Shows some understanding of studio or project concept.	All instructions followed. Basic use of problem-solving skills. Shows understanding of studio or project concept.	All instructions followed. Exceptional use of problem-solving skills. Shows notable creativity and originality in using the studio or project concept.

1 Insuficiente	**2 Aceptable**	**3 Bueno**	**4 Excelente**
No ha seguido las instrucciones. No se ha esforzado en resolver los problemas. No demuestra comprensión del concepto del taller o del proyecto.	Ha seguido algunas instrucciones, pero no todas. Demuestra algún esfuerzo en resolver los problemas. Demuestra alguna comprensión del concepto del taller o del proyecto.	Ha seguido todas las instrucciones. Demuestra un uso básico de destrezas de resolución de problemas. Demuestra comprensión del concepto del taller o del proyecto.	Ha seguido todas las instrucciones. Demuestra un uso excepcional de destrezas de resolución de problemas. Demuestra destacada creatividad y originalidad al aplicar el concepto del taller o del proyecto.

Name _____

Unit 6 Self-Check

Unit Concepts

1. The art career that I found most interesting was _____ because

   _____

   _____.

2. I want to learn more about the art career _____ because

   _____

   _____.

Studios and Portfolio Project

3. Which studio/project was the most difficult? Why?

   _____

4. What would you do differently next time?

   _____

5. Which studio/project was the most creative for expressing your ideas?

   _____

6. What unit concepts helped you with the studios/project?

   _____

7. What did you learn from creating the artworks in this unit?

   _____

8. What technique would you like to explore further?

   _____

Unidad 6 Autoevaluación

Conceptos de la unidad

1. La profesión artística que me pareció más interesante fue _____

porque _____

_____

2. Quiero informarme mejor sobre la profesión de _____

porque _____

_____

Talleres y proyecto para el portafolio

3. ¿Qué taller o proyecto fue el más difícil? ¿Por qué?

_____

4. ¿Qué harías de manera diferente la próxima vez?

_____

5. ¿Qué taller o proyecto te permitió expresar tus ideas de manera más creativa?

_____

6. ¿Qué conceptos aprendidos en esta unidad te sirvieron de ayuda para realizar los talleres o el proyecto?

_____

7. ¿Qué aprendiste al crear tus obras de arte de esta unidad?

_____

8. ¿Qué técnica te gustaría explorar más?

_____

Curriculum Connection

Research

Materials
☐ computer with Internet access
☐ printer

Form and Function of Headgear Explain that throughout history hats have been worn for protection and to make a fashion statement. Have students work together in small groups to research different hat styles in different cultures. Each group can choose several hats and provide a picture and description of each, including its use, historical timeframe, social or economic connections, and so on. Use the hat notes to create a bulletin board display. Remember to guide students in using safe Internet practices. ⓢ

Math

Materials
☐ tape measure or yardstick and meter stick
☐ measuring items such as paper clips, erasers, index cards, shoes
☐ pens, pencils, writing paper

Measure It Discuss the importance of taking accurate measurements when designing an installation. Have students measure the classroom using standard and metric units. Then have small groups work together to create measurement systems using their own units of measurement, such as a paper clip or shoe. Students can use their unit of measurement to measure the classroom and report their results. Have students use their different units to create an equivalency chart.

Music

Materials
☐ students' projects from Studio 6
☐ pens, pencils, writing paper

Advertising Jingles Have students work independently to write advertising jingles for the everyday product they created in Studio 6. Their jingles should be a catchy but accurate way to describe the product's function and advantages. Students can perform their jingles for the class while displaying their everyday products.

Physical Education

Materials
☐ health textbooks
☐ posterboard
☐ rulers
☐ pencils, pens, water-based markers

Fitness Fun Storyboard Have students work in pairs to create a storyboard to teach their classmates how to be physically fit. The storyboards should illustrate exercises such as jumping jacks, toe touches, leg raises, and sit-ups. Pairs can trade completed storyboards and use them to demonstrate each other's fitness fun program.

Culminating Activities

Museum Project: Comparing and Contrasting Applied Arts and Fine Arts

Take students to an art museum or on a virtual tour to learn more about careers in art. For a virtual tour, see the Web site for The Getty Museum **(www.getty.edu).** Remember to guide students in using safe Internet practices. ⑤

Before You Go

Remind students what they learned in previous Museum Projects. Then discuss the importance of using their time wisely when they visit a real or virtual museum to get the most from the experience. Tell students that they will visit a real or a virtual museum to find out more about applied and fine arts, as well as about art careers.

During the Visit

Review the characteristics of applied arts and fine arts.

- Ask each student to find several examples of applied arts, such as furniture, costume designs, or architecture. Have students repeat the process with fine arts to identify drawings, paintings, and sculptures.
- Have students create a two-column chart. In column one, they should list the title, artist, and description of examples of applied art. In column two, they can list the same information for examples of fine art.
- Have students analyze similarities and differences between applied artworks and fine artworks.

When You Return

Have students use their charts to share information about the artworks they saw and discuss how each form of art serves a specific function in our lives.

Performing Arts: Community Tour

After students complete Studio 4 on page 267, have them create a gallery and give tours.

Prepare

Divide the class into small groups and have group members follow these steps:

- Display the Postmodern facades in areas of the classroom to create a Postmodern community.
- Confer with other group members to specify the unique and useful function that each building fulfills within the community.
- Write a brief speech that describes their building, its Postmodern elements, and its uses in the community.

Practice

Have students practice their speeches for smooth delivery and eye contact with the audience.

Perform

Have groups give guided tours of the community to classmates, with group members delivering speeches that describe their buildings.

Studio/Project Log

Record the students' scores for each Studio and Portfolio Project activity

	Names																			
Studio 1																				
Studio 2																				
Studio 3																				
Studio 4																				
Studio 5																				
Studio 6																				
Studio 7																				
Studio 8																				
Studio 9																				
Portfolio Project																				
Studio 1																				
Studio 2																				
Studio 3																				
Studio 4																				
Studio 5																				
Studio 6																				
Studio 7																				
Portfolio Project																				
Studio 1																				
Studio 2																				
Studio 3																				
Studio 4																				
Studio 5																				
Studio 6																				
Studio 7																				
Studio 8																				
Studio 9																				
Studio 10																				
Portfolio Project																				

Studio/Project Log

		Names																	
Unit 4	Studio 1																			
	Studio 2																			
	Studio 3																			
	Studio 4																			
	Studio 5																			
	Studio 6																			
	Studio 7																			
	Studio 8																			
	Portfolio Project																			
Unit 5	Studio 1																			
	Studio 2																			
	Studio 3																			
	Studio 4																			
	Studio 5																			
	Studio 6																			
	Studio 7																			
	Studio 8																			
	Studio 9																			
	Studio 10																			
	Portfolio Project																			
Unit 6	Studio 1																			
	Studio 2																			
	Studio 3																			
	Studio 4																			
	Studio 5																			
	Studio 6																			
	Studio 7																			
	Studio 8																			
	Portfolio Project																			

Venn Diagram

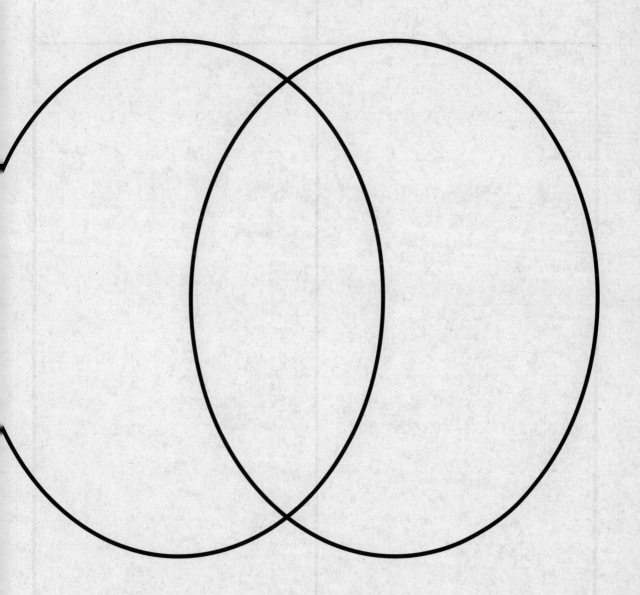

Two-Column Chart

Three-Column Chart

Flowchart

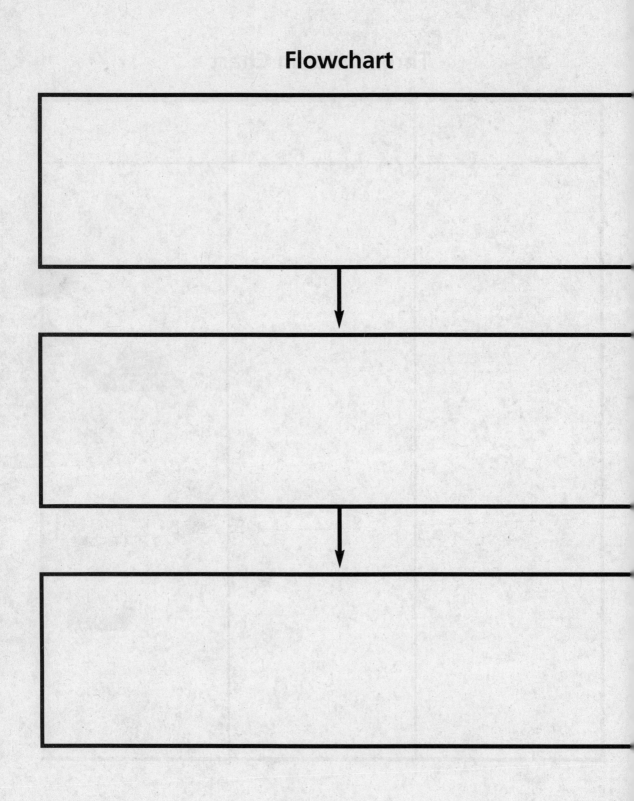